THE DOG ATE MY RESUMÉ

SURVIVAL TIPS FOR LIFE AFTER COLLEGE

ZACK ARNSTEIN, CLASS OF '02
LARRY ARNSTEIN, CLASS OF '67

SANTA
MONICA
PRESS

S A N T A
M O N I C A
P R E S S

Published by:
Santa Monica Press LLC
P.O. Box 1076
Santa Monica, CA 90406-1076
1-800-784-9553
www.santamonicapress.com
books@santamonicapress.com

Printed in the United States

Santa Monica Press books are available at special quantity discounts when purchased in bulk by corporations, organizations, or groups. Please call our Special Sales department at 1-800-784-9553.

Library of Congress Cataloging-in-Publication Data

Arnstein, Zack, 1980–
        The dog ate my resume: survival tips for life after college / Zack Arnstein, Larry Arnstein.—1st ed.
        p. cm.
        Includes bibliographical references and index.
        ISBN 1-891661-37-X
        1. Conduct of life—Humor. 2. Career development—Humor. 3. College graduates—Humor. I. Arnstein, Larry, 1945- II. Title.
        PN6231.C6142A76 2004
        818'.607—dc22

                                                                        2004000452

Cover and Interior design by Lynda "Cool Dog" Jakovich

CONTENTS

8   **Introduction**

9   **Section One: Plundering the Resources at Your College**

10   **Chapter 1:** Not the Introduction

13   **Chapter 2:** Making Your Major Your Springboard to the Future

15   **Chapter 3:** The Career Guidance Center: Finding It, or Are You Prepared for the Next Exciting Chapter in Your Life?

19   **Chapter 4:** Identifying, Finding and Cornering Your Faculty Advisor

21   **Chapter 5:** Keys to Graduating: Completing Your Course Work and Alternate Suggestions

21   **Chapter 6:** Job Fairs: Bring Your Own Booze, but in a Plain Brown Bag

21   **Chapter 7:** Winning Interview Techniques: Developing a Go-Getter Attitude, or at Least Faking One

154   **Chapter 8:** Staying in School for Advanced Studies: Grad School, or Just Refusing to Leave Your Dorm

30   **Chapter 9:** Resumé Do's and Don'ts: A Few Years in Prison for a Felony is Not Necessarily a Bad Thing

33   **Chapter 10:** Letters of Recommendation: 10 Ways to Find Out Who Will Give You a Good One

39   **Chapter 11:** Surviving Graduation Day: You Are the Future—Stop Slouching

42   **A Few Final Words of Encouragement**

43 **Section Two: Leaving College—Your Personal Journey Through Hell**

44 **Chapter 12:** Inspirational Quotes

47 **Chapter 13:** Prioritizing Your Decision-Making: What is the Meaning of Life, or Where Will I Sleep Tonight?

50 **Chapter 14:** Navigating and Guiding Your Family Discussions About What You Will Do After College, Including Good Answers to the Big Question— Truthful and Otherwise

57 **Chapter 15:** Networking (With All Your Slacker Friends)

62 **Chapter 16:** Your Own Apartment vs. Living at Home: Comparing Apples and Oranges (Both of Which Are Only Available at Home)

70 **Chapter 17:** Managing Your Finances: How Many Credit Cards is Not Enough?

73 **Chapter 18:** A Word About Pets (Avoid)

76 **Chapter 19:** You Don't Have Time to Read This Chapter

77 **Chapter 20:** Navigating and Guiding Your Family Discussions About What Your Child Will Do After College—A Study Guide for Parents (Students: Skip This at Your Own Risk)

81 **Chapter 21:** Essential Real World Survivor Skills, or How to Get Selected to Be on *The Real World* or *Survivor*

81 **Chapter 22:** A Tourist's Guide to the Real World: Knowing How You're Doing Without Grades

85 **Section Three: Choosing a Career by Process of Elimination**

86 Career Elimination Exercise

88 **Chapter 23:** The Military: Getting Accepted into the Military Services is Not That Difficult!

92 **Chapter 24:** Fabulous Careers, or Careers in Fabulousness

54 **Chapter 25:** Law: You Don't Have to Be a Lawyer to Make a Living Suing Other People!

96 **Chapter 26:** Careers in Computers: Fatal Error E06#58647 Has Occurred

99 **Chapter 27:** Education: Long Summer Vacations, Plus the Chance to Make Someone as Miserable as Your Teachers Made You

102 **Chapter 28:** A Career in Law Enforcement: Do You Have Any Idea How Fast You Were Reading?

106 **Chapter 29:** Careers in Psychology & Counseling: Hanging Around with People Even More Screwed Up Than You

110 **Chapter 30:** A Career in Show Business

114 **Chapter 31:** Starting a Band: Why Not Just Roll Around Naked on Broken Glass?

120 **Chapter 32:** Professional Sports: Pros and Cons of Leaving College Before You've Completed All Four Years of Remedial Reading

123 **Chapter 33:** Dream Jobs: Getting Paid for What You Do Anyway

126 **Chapter 34:** Crime: The Most Lucrative Profession for Which There Are No Formal Requirements

129 **Chapter 35:** Careers in Religion: Buy 10 More Copies of This Book and Your Sins Are Forgiven

133 **Chapter 36:** A Career in Editing: Do We Really Need This Chapter?

135 Mid Term Exam

139   **Section Four: Choosing a Real Job on the Basis of What You Can Actually Get**

140   **Chapter 37:** Not Peaking Too Soon

27   **Chapter 38:** Bartending: Listening to Drunks, but This Time Getting Paid for It

143   **Chapter 39:** Internships: Why Settle for Underpaid When You Can Be Not Paid at All?

147   **Chapter 40:** Doing Nothing

151   **Chapter 41:** Waiting Tables: It's Not Rocket Science, but the Tips are Better

158   **Chapter 42:** Winning the Lottery: Somebody Has to Win, Why Not You?

161   **Chapter 43:** Messenger Service: At Least You're Not in Some Office

161   **Chapter 44:** Begging: Being Your Own Boss While Working Outdoors—It Could Be Worse

164   **Chapter 45:** Telemarketing: Could Not Be Worse

118   **Chapter 46:** Temp Work: Not So Great, but It's Only Temporary!

166   **Chapter 47:** The Classifieds: Now You're Desperate

169   **Chapter 48:** Online Job Searching: You Can Be Humiliated in the Comfort of Your Own Home

171   **Chapter 49:** Careers in Research: Body Parts You Can Live Without

173   **Section Five: Community Service: If All Else Fails, Help the Needy**

174   **Chapter 50:** The Peace Corps: 10 Diseases You've Never Even Heard Of

175   **Chapter 51:** AmeriCorps: 10 Lethal Weapons You've Never Heard Of

176   **Chapter 52:** Making the World a Better Place, or at Least Cleaning Your Apartment

178   **Final Exam**

181   **Appendix**

182   Full Life Experience Check List

184   How to Succeed in Life: Writing Impressive Class Notes for the Alumni Magazine

187   The Individually Customized, Nondenominationally Specific Holiday Networking Card Template

188   Index

INTRODUCTION

Of all the many bad things about Introductions, the worst is that the pages *don't even count!* You could read a 20- to 30-page Introduction, and then turn the page only to find that you haven't even *started* reading, because all the Introduction pages were numbered with things like "iv" and "vii" and "xviii"! And you don't hit *page* one until *chapter* one begins!

For that reason (among others), the Hell with the Introduction. You know what this book is about, right?

Right?

You bought it, didn't you?

OK, so you didn't buy it. Somebody gave it to you. But at least you're reading it. So if you don't know what the book is about, you're in even worse shape than we thought, which is why you definitely need to stop wasting your time on the Introduction.

(However, to show you just what kind of a great book this is, you *will* be given credit for reading the Introduction, Title Page, Copyright Page, and also the Table of Contents. Chapter One starts on page ten!)

SECTION ONE

PLUNDERING THE RESOURCES AT YOUR COLLEGE

CHAPTER 1:

NOT THE INTRODUCTION

Now that the Best Years of Your Life are nearly over, the time has come to think about your future, something you've been **putting off**, or they wouldn't have been the Best Years of Your Life.

We have simplified our message as much as possible by dividing essential information you will need into ☺ Good News and ☹ Bad News aspects of the various topics under discussion. For example, you will learn the Bad News that your life has already **peaked**, and the trajectory from here on out is a gentle downward spiral (see Fig. 1), or possibly an abrupt plunge into the abyss (see Fig. 2). This may come as a surprise, especially if you did not realize these past four years have been the happiest ones in your life.

Sorry.

Fig. 1

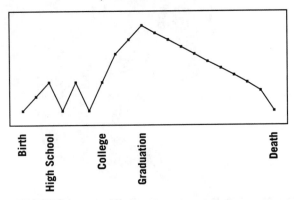

Life Trajectory A:
Gentle Downward Spiral
(Recommended)

Fig. 2

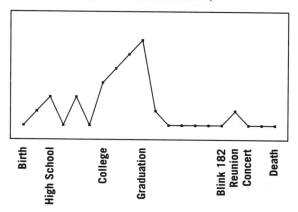

Life Trajectory B:
Abrupt Plunge
(Not Recommended)

However, there is also the Good News that your life is **not over**. In fact there are many years ahead of you, years which must be filled up with stuff. This book will help you fill up your life with stuff!

Because graduation and the subsequent rest-of-life experience is a family process (and taking full advantage of the multi-generational perspective of the authors), each chapter has a **Summary for Parents** and a **Summary for Students**, except for those that don't.

To guide you through the sometimes unfamiliar territory covered in this book, we provide comforting, familiar exercises you can participate in like frequent **tests** you can cheat on easily. These tests are also a reminder for students that even after college:

→ you will be constantly judged,

and a reminder for parents that

→ you are never too old to fail.

In addition, there are helpful **questionnaires** to guide you as you identify your strengths and weaknesses, and in-depth analyses of various career options open to you. There is also a Table of Contents and an Index which can help you find the information most relevant to your skills and interests. For example, if you're interested in **acting**, you may want to skip directly to the chapter on **Waiting Tables**. Also, you will be pleased to see that the text has already been **highlighted** for your convenience, so you can **skim**!

If you're confused by any of the symbols used in the text, you can refer to the following Legend:

LEGEND

Bold ....Pay particular attention to this **key concept**.

Italics............This is a *key concept* that you should pay particular attention to.

★ ....Paying attention particularly to ★ this is key to understanding the concept.

→ ....Hey! You should really pay attention to → this!

♌................Your kitchen is on fire.

☺ ....This person is on drugs.

☹ ....This person is also on drugs, but of a lower quality than ☺ this person.

SUMMARY FOR STUDENTS

Oh, so you skipped right to the Chapter Summary, huh? Well, at least that proves you learned *something* in college.

SUMMARY FOR PARENTS

If you're still looking at this book in the bookstore and haven't yet decided to buy it, be assured that there will be no further reference to the offensive subject of drug use on campus. So go ahead and buy the book. Unless you liked the drug reference, in which case you can be assured there will be several more references to the offensive but hilarious subject of drug use on campus. You should also buy the book.

CHAPTER 2:

Making Your Major Your Springboard to the Future

Yes, you *do* have a major. Take as much time as you need to remember what it is. This is the field of study you have chosen for serious focus and concentration. But what career path has your major prepared you for? (or if you're an English Major, what is the career path for which your Major has prepared you?)[1] Here is a quick checklist to acquaint you with some of the exciting possibilities:

Major/Career Opportunity Checklist

Major	Career Opportunity
Sociology & Religious Studies	Waiter
Anthropology & Comparative Philosophy	Waiter
Algebraic Number Theory	Bartender
History	Further study in another field
Chemical Engineering	Shouldn't you already have a job?
English Literature	House sitter

---

[1] **Warning** to English Majors: in the Real World, nobody cares if you end a sentence with a preposition. In fact, if you try too hard to avoid it, bullies will stomp on you and beat your head in.

Major	Career Opportunity
Italian Literature	Pizza delivery
Ecology & Global Environment	Telemarketer
Political Science	Volunteer
Psychology	Fortune teller
Creative Writing	Parking attendant
Women's Studies	Waitress

Of course, this is only a rough guideline. If, for example, you majored in Ecology & Global Environment, there's really no reason you can't aspire to become a House Sitter, even though that profession is more closely associated with English Lit majors.

SUMMARY FOR STUDENTS

Within any academic discipline, there are multiple career paths one may take. Except in Art History, where there are only two career paths: teaching and cleaning the floors in an art museum.

SUMMARY FOR PARENTS

You just sat there and watched while your child got a degree in Art History??

CHAPTER 3:

THE CAREER GUIDANCE CENTER: FINDING IT, OR ARE YOU PREPARED FOR THE NEXT EXCITING CHAPTER IN YOUR LIFE?

You may not realize it, but you've been attending classes these past four years. During this time you have been accumulating, quietly but steadily, the life skills and maturity you need to participate in what is called the Real World! (Not the TV show, which takes a lot more serious preparation.)

"When," you may ask, "did all this happen?"

Not during your routine, day-to-day life at college, that's for sure. Rather, it was while you were performing those boring tasks which actually *interfered* with your undergraduate life. Yes, it was those dreary hours taking notes in class, studying, writing papers and taking exams. Who knew?

These tedious distractions, useful mainly to mark time between parties and other more important activities, are surprisingly what will lead to your becoming a degree-carrying college graduate!

But before taking that first, bracing plunge into the lung-seizing, icy waters of Real Life, your very first step will be to schedule an interview at the Career Guidance Center.

In order to schedule this interview, you must *find* the Career Guidance Center. This is not easy, since the location is a secret.

Step 1: Don't waste your time asking your classmates: nobody knows where the Career Guidance Center is.

Step 2: Go to the Dean's Office, and get a college catalog.

Step 3: Turn to the extensive material found inside it, directed at your parents, about how much Career Guidance you've been getting during your undergraduate years. (Be careful not to disrupt the quiet dignity of the Dean's Office by laughing hysterically and rolling around on the floor.) Somewhere in this section is the **secret location** of the Career Guidance Center.

When you have found it, you will be surprised to find that it is open! It is always open. It is open at night, on weekends and holidays, in the summer, during national emergencies, always, always open. This is because of the Career Guidance Counselors' pathetically hopeful belief that if it is convenient for the students, they will find the Center and take advantage of it.

The first question you will want to ask is: are there any job openings at the Career Guidance Center? Since working at the Center means you would continue to enjoy all the many benefits of being in college without having to pay tuition, attend classes, write papers and take exams, this is one of the world's **best jobs**. Also, since nobody ever goes there, it is one of the world's easiest jobs, consisting primarily of writing about all the career guidance which is provided to the undergraduates, for publication in the College Catalog. Consequently, there are not any openings, but it can't hurt to ask.

To help the Career Guidance Counselor learn more about your potential, you will be asked to fill out something like the following:

CAREER APTITUDE QUESTIONNAIRE

1. You would consider a job in which
A) Your starting salary was modest, but there was opportunity for advancement.
B) Long hours were required at first, but eventually you could move up.
C) You must wear clothes to start with, but after a while clothing is optional.

2. You are fluent in
A) English, Spanish, French, Japanese and Russian.
B) English, German, Italian, Portuguese.
C) English as a Second Language.

3. You are a person who regularly thinks
A) Outside the box.
B) Inside the box, but with a good view of outside.
C) Under the box.
D) Jack in the Box.

4. If the Career Guidance Center counselors know so much about finding great careers, how come they're still working at the Career Guidance Center?
A) Don't be a little snot. They're just trying to help.

Answer these questions **truthfully**, and in a manner which presents your best qualities, even if you have to **lie**.

If after considering the advice you receive from the Center, you're still unsure about what career path is right for you, you may want to ask: "What are last year's graduates doing?"

Fortunately, the Center keeps excellent records, as you can see in this helpful chart:

What Last Year's Graduates Are Doing

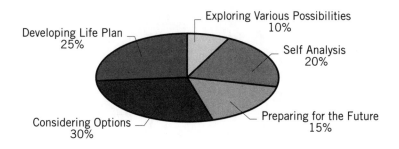

Exploring Various Possibilities
10%

Developing Life Plan
25%

Self Analysis
20%

Considering Options
30%

Preparing for the Future
15%

SUMMARY FOR STUDENTS

Ah, screw it. You don't want to spend any of your valuable, remaining college time doing unrequired thinking at the Career Guidance Center. On the other hand, if you walk into the Center, say "hello," and immediately leave, you can tell anyone (your parents) that you've been there, you spoke to a counselor, and it really wasn't all that helpful.

SUMMARY FOR PARENTS

Your graduate is totally ready for the world! He/she has received *tons* of Career Guidance, a *fabulous* education, and will hit the ground running, probably right back into your house. Not to worry, your hatchling will take wing just as soon as she/he decides on which one of those terrific job offers to accept. Be patient, this make take a few years.

CHAPTER 4:

Identifying, Finding and Cornering Your Faculty Advisor

You may be surprised to discover that you have one—a respected professor who is supposed to have been following your college career closely, so that she can guide and direct your efforts in choosing the right courses, shape your academic life with an eye to your future, while nurturing your talents and ambitions.

This person has been **hiding** from you, but by following our easy-to-use techniques, she can be identified and cornered.

1. Break into the Dean's Office at night, find the Secret Files. (Look under: "Files, Secret." If that doesn't work, try "Secret: Files.") Anyway, somewhere in there you'll find the name of your Faculty Advisor.

2. Call this person on the phone, pretending to be a High Official of the MacArthur Genius Awards Panel, the one that gives people lots of money, with no strings attached, to do whatever they want to do, simply for being a genius.

3. Have the "High Official" arrange a lunch meeting with your Advisor at a nearby restaurant, to discuss details of the MacArthur Genius Grant. Your Advisor will probably show up early, not wanting to miss this appointment, and you can be pretty sure she will be in a good mood.

4. Be waiting at the restaurant, and act real surprised to see your Advisor. You could break the ice by saying, "Say, aren't you my Advisor?" You then introduce yourself. Because she

is in such a good mood, waiting for the imminent arrival of her Genius Grant, she will not go into the pattern of **evasive action** normally used to avoid student advisees. In fact, she will probably be inclined to sit down with you for a few minutes, and give you some **actual advice**.

SUMMARY FOR STUDENTS

Wow. That was a pretty short chapter!

SUMMARY FOR PARENTS

It's really comforting to know that even though you can't be at college to avoid giving your child the guidance he so desperately needs, there is another, competent adult right on campus who can be counted on to avoid this responsibility in your absence.

(If you insist on knowing what happened to Chapters 5 & 6, see Chapter 36: A Career in Editing.)

CHAPTER 7:

WINNING INTERVIEW TECHNIQUES: DEVELOPING A GO-GETTER ATTITUDE, OR AT LEAST FAKING ONE

In case you didn't make it to the Career Guidance Center ☹, the essential advice on interview techniques you would have received there is provided here ☺.

The most common mistake job seekers make is to freak out before the interview and try to reinvent themselves as someone they're not. It is in your best interest to present yourself as you actually are, unless of course, "who you are" is a person who is essentially **unemployable**. In that case, you should definitely re-invent yourself as somebody else. In any event, the interview should have the feel of a conversation between friends.

DO

☺ Have a few drinks before the interview, it will help you relax. Remember, you're funnier and better looking after a couple of Irish Car Bombs.

☺ Talk about yourself in the third person. It will **hammer** your name into your interviewer's head and create a strong impression. "Johnny Murdock wants to work for your company! Johnny Murdock doesn't take 'no' for an answer!"

DON'T

☹ Apologize or make excuses. For example, being **fashionably late** to an interview is not necessarily bad. Depend on your **self-confidence** to see you through this situation—your interviewer will be impressed. To add to this air of self confidence:

DO

☺ Chew gum.

☺ If you smoke, be sure and offer one to your potential employer, especially if you are in his office.

☺ A firm, strong handshake is a must. This is your moment to demonstrate your physical strength. Squeeze until your interviewer winces in pain; that way, you can be sure you've made a ★ **strong** ★ impression!

DON'T

☹ Mumble. Never assume your interviewer can hear you. Pick a point ten feet **behind** your interviewer and **project** to that point. It's always better to speak too loudly than not loudly enough.

DO

☺ Constantly ask about money—it will show your ambition.

☺ If you've had an unpleasant work experience, talk about your desire to kill your last boss—it will show you expect to be well-treated.

DON'T

☹ Get stressed out. If you're starting to get stressed out, count to 10 **out loud**, and start the interview over again, with that firm, strong handshake.

A valuable employee is someone who has **specialized** skills or knowledge not commonly held. But don't ☹ just blurt it out. Work it into the conversation in a ☺ **subtle** way:

> INTERVIEWER
> It's nice to meet you.

> YOU
> I can make a powerful nuclear bomb in my basement.

☺ A good subject to raise in your first interview is vacations: how much paid vacation time will there be? Can you take more if you need it? Does the company need to know exactly when you are returning from vacation, in terms of a specific date? Would your vacation time be in addition to religious holidays like Christmas week and Mardi Gras? This shows you are **thinking ahead**.

TRICK QUESTIONS

Sometimes interviewers will try to trip you up by asking trick questions. Don't fall into the trap by trying to answer them. Instead have ready retorts prepared ahead of time. This way, you are in control, not them.

Trick Question	Ready Retort
Why do want this job?	Why do you care?
Why don't you tell me a little more about your employment history?	Why don't you ask me another question?
What do you like to do in your spare time?	I respectfully refuse to answer that question in accordance with the 5th Amendment to the Constitution of the United States.

Your potential employer now knows you can't be manipulated, which was the point of the trick questions to begin with.

DRUG TEST

Some employers will insist you take a drug test. In order to prepare for this possibility,

→ you should know whether or not you're on drugs. ←

This may not be as easy as it seems, especially if you *are* on drugs. If you're not sure, here's a simple pre-test you can take to find out.

1. Chevy Chase is:
A) Hysterical, always.
B) Pretty darn funny in the three *National Lampoon Vacation* movies.
C) Not funny at all.

2. That noise outside was:
A) A government spy chopper.
B) The police, probably.
C) Just your cat scratching at the window.

3. We were just talking about:
A) Um...
B) No, wait, wasn't it...?
C) That noise outside.

4. This flower is: 🌻
A) A California Fawn Lily.
B) Just a crude drawing.
C) A celebration of the eternal oneness of the life force throughout the universe.

ANSWER KEY

If you actually watched all three *National Lampoon Vacation* movies, you're definitely on drugs.

If it turns out you're on drugs, drinking a bottle of vodka is known to flush your system of dangerous substances which can show up on these tests.

ADVANCED INTERVIEW TECHNIQUES

When applying for a management position, or a job in the corporate sector, you must present yourself as an important business personality, for whom time is money, etc. To accomplish this, have a friend call you in the middle of your interview, and stage a conversation like this:

EMPLOYER
Tell me a bit more about your qualifications.

YOU
Well you see—(ring) excuse me—(answer phone). Talk to me.

YOUR FRIEND
What's up, you wanted me to call you?

YOU
Well tell him he can start looking for a job somewhere else, then.

YOUR FRIEND
What are you talking about?

YOU
600? No! I need at least 900 and by this afternoon.

YOUR FRIEND
900 what?

YOU
That's right, and reschedule my appointment with the investor group for Thursday.

YOUR FRIEND
I'm hanging up. (click)

YOU
All right, no more calls for an hour.

The dynamic has certainly changed. With all the charisma and confidence you've displayed in your interview, your potential employer may be asking *you* for a job.

SUMMARY FOR STUDENTS

The main thing is to be remembered. You can accomplish this by something as simple as wearing a **large hat**.

SUMMARY FOR PARENTS

Chevy Chase is actually a very talented comic actor, and you don't have to consume **massive quantities of drugs** to appreciate his art.

(OK, so your interview didn't go so well. But we don't want you to get discouraged, so we're pulling an Emergency Chapter from one of our Advanced Sections: Jobs You Can Actually Get.)

CHAPTER 38:

BARTENDING: LISTENING TO DRUNKS, BUT THIS TIME GETTING PAID FOR IT

If you've wasted your precious college years drinking, you may want to take advantage of your expertise by applying for a job as a bartender. It must be said that this career choice will probably not be popular with your parents, who've gone deeply into debt so that you could go to college and not have to work as a bartender. But if this is what you want, remember: this is *your* life, not theirs. It is crucial to your future happiness and self respect to take charge of your own life and, ultimately, your parents will respect you more for it. So approach them firmly, with affection and gratitude for all that they have given you, but determined to be your own man or woman, and lie.

"Yes," we hear you asking, "but ethically speaking, exactly what kind of lie?" It really doesn't matter. Tell them anything but the truth. They are not ready, at this delicate moment, for the truth, or as Jack Nicholson put it in that movie you watched instead of studying, they "can't handle the truth." Perhaps at a later time, to be determined at a later date, they will be ready.

If you're lucky enough to have brothers and sisters, let *them* take the heat. If they are successful and make your parents proud, they will relieve pressure on you by giving the folks a son/daughter to brag about—if they are worse screwups than you are, a solid career as a bartender will begin to look a lot better.

There will be critics who sneer (it's the only facial expression critics are capable of forming) that "bartending" and "career" are words which do not belong in the same sentence. Your comeback to these critics can be: "Oh, yeah?" or possibly: "Sez who?" or more effectively: "So's your Momma!" Anyway, the world of bartending is not subject to the whims of critics, which is one of the advantages of a career in bartending.

But not the only one.

Advantages of Career in Bartending	**Disadvantages of Career in Bartending**
☺ You don't have to get up early in the morning.	☹ You have to stay up very, very late.
☺ Meet lots of people.	☹ Most of them are drunks.
☺ Hear interesting stories.	☹ The stories aren't really that interesting.
☺ Listen to the latest dance music while you work.	☹ Over and over and over again.

But whatever the advantages and disadvantages may be, bartending is, after all, a job, and you will be paid for it, in addition to which, if you get the drink orders right some of the time, you will get **tips**. ☺

VOCABULARY ALERT

A **tip** is the alcoholic's way of personally thanking you for contributing to his life-consuming addiction.

Remember, you can always say you're learning about the world, and about human nature, and booze, all of which are important for whatever you end up doing with the rest of your life, especially if it happens to be tending bar.

SUMMARY FOR STUDENTS

If you don't have a job, you're probably spending most of your time there, anyway. If you're going to *be* at a bar, you might as well *work* at a bar.

SUMMARY FOR PARENTS

Lots of adventurous kids tend bar for a while after college to get a taste of what it's like to tend bar. This doesn't necessarily mean your kid has wasted four years of very expensive college classes. For all you know, your kid didn't even *go* to classes.

SPECIAL BONUS SECTION FOR DRUGGIES

If you misunderstood the phrase "higher education," and wasted your precious college years taking drugs, don't feel left out. You may qualify for the job of Drug Counselor. This can be an excellent job, and there is no better Drug Counselor than one who has Been There and Back, something you should emphasize in your resumé (ALERT: for this job ONLY!), but in a responsible and cautious manner. If, for example, your most recent experience with recreational drugs was last night, it would be more prudent to say something like: your experimentation with drugs is "in the past," a "**youthful mistake**" which you "**deeply regret**." The experience does qualify you to relate to what a drug abuser is going through, and will enable you to gain their trust, and help them. Also, working in a Rehab Center will place you in a working environment where you'll be surrounded by peers and colleagues with similar interests and life goals. (And they can help you score.)

(If you insist on reading Chapter 8, go to page 154, but you're not being very flexible. Life is not as orderly as college. You might as well get used to it.)

CHAPTER 9:

RESUMÉ DO'S & DON'TS: A FEW YEARS IN PRISON FOR A FELONY IS NOT NECESSARILY A BAD THING

Your resumé is your calling card, so it's important to have a good one. Just because your actual life and work experience may be somewhat uninspiring doesn't mean your resumé must be.

Here are a few examples of how to take your uninspiring actual experiences and transform them into resumé gold.

Reality	Resumé Gold
☹ You've never worked a day in your life.	☺ Never been terminated by an an employer.
☹ You have a serious drug addiction.	☺ Experience with suppliers maintaining consistent inventory levels in differing demand environments.
☹ You slept through all your classes.	☺ Outstanding achievement in multitasking.

PRACTICAL HINTS

Do Customize Your Resumé

If you are applying for a job as, say, a bouncer at a bar, you'll want to include any past convictions you may have on your record for assault and battery. Do NOT, however, include this part of your history on your application for ANY OTHER JOB.

Similarly, if you're applying for a job as a preschool teacher, you may want to list the many hours you've spent playing in the sand box with your little friends. On the other hand, do NOT include this on your application for your job as a bouncer. (Also, do NOT include this on your application to seminary.)

Don't Generalize

In order to customize your resumé properly, you must do your homework in researching the company where you're applying. While that conviction for **petty theft** should be omitted from your resumé when applying to *most* companies, if you're applying to any Wall Street brokerage, you should describe it as: entry-level experience in **aggressive business practice**. Just be sure, in any subsequent interview, to say how deeply you regret being caught.

Do Include Special Awards and Recognitions

You do have them, somewhere, and it's especially important to include them if you have **nothing else** to put on your resumé. Just go into your closet and haul out that old box with all the ribbons that say "Participant" on them. You probably wouldn't have them if they didn't really represent some kind of prize, probably **First Prize**. Many of them may not have any further information on them, so you have to think back to what they were for. Again, most probably they were for something like: "Outstanding Achievement in Service to the Community," or "Accomplishment in Academic Excellence." Anyway, how can you be sure they weren't for that if they don't say anything but "Participant"? You can't, so you may as well put in that other stuff.

Do Use Abbreviations

Your six months residence at the New Jersey State Prison in Trenton can easily be restated as: Six months with N.J.S.P. in Trenton. Sounds better, doesn't it?

How to Organize Your Resumé

There are four ways to organize your resumé: **chronological** (by date, in order), **functional** (your skills and interests), **chrono-functional** (combination of the first two), and **periodical** (by what **bands** you liked at the time).

Making Your Resumé Longer

An absolute minimum length for your resumé is one page. If work experience and double spacing aren't enough, feel free to talk about yourself a little: you know, what movies you like, your turn-ons and turn-offs, etc. Like:

"I used to work at Domino's, I've seen *American Pie, Two* 12 times, I have a signed copy of every album **Iron Maiden** ever made, I like long walks along the beach, and being tied up and whipped. I *don't* like phony pickup lines or domestic violence."

You see how much you've added to the length and quality of your resumé? Now your potential employer really knows you, and your resumé will stand out in the crowd.

SUMMARY FOR STUDENTS

Don't misspell the word "resumé" on your resumé. If you're having trouble finding the accent mark function on your word processing program, try smashing your computer with your fist, then throwing it on the ground and jumping up and down on it in a fit of violent rage.

SUMMARY FOR PARENTS

Remember, your failure as a parent is not reflected in your son or daughter's resumé. It's reflected in *your* resumé.

CHAPTER 10:

LETTERS OF RECOMMENDATION: 10 WAYS TO FIND OUT WHO WILL GIVE YOU A GOOD ONE

VOCABULARY ALERT

A **letter of recommendation** is an essay about you by someone who knows you well, which is also a work of **fiction**.

Therefore, the best person to write one, other than yourself, is a person with a highly developed creative **imagination** and a poorly developed sense of **ethics**.

But which professor to choose?

To answer this question, you must approach potential candidates and engage them in casual conversation. Here is a sample dialogue you can examine for hints: You see your target, the distinguished Professor Warmdockler, grading papers at an outdoor table by the Student Union.

YOU

Professor Warmdockler!

PROF. W

(looking up)
Do I know you?   ← *Considering your record, promising start*

> YOU

YOUR NAME HERE, from your Society & Religions class!

> PROF. W

I don't teach a Society & Religions class.

> YOU

Right, right. I meant that *other* class.

← *Decent recovery*

> PROF. W

Economic Development in South America?

> YOU

That's the one. I love that class!

> PROF. W

Funny, I don't recall your name.

← *Excellent*

> YOU

Oh, that's because I changed it midway through the semester. I had a religious experience. Anyway, I was wondering—

> PROF. W

Are you sure you're in my class?

> YOU

I wrote that paper on the Oil Industry in Venezuela.

> PROF. W

Ah, now I remember. An excellent paper!

← *This is good*

> YOU

(modestly)
Well, I did put some extra effort into it.

> PROF. W

Of course I'm a bit prejudiced, since it was my Master's Thesis. Tell me, how did you find it?

← *This is very bad*

YOU

It's one of the best papers on the internet. Everyone says so.

PROF. W:

How flattering. I hope you'll tell that to the Plagiarism Committee next week. Now what was it you wanted?

YOU

Oh, look at the time! Well, it's been nice chatting with you, gotta run!

OK. So maybe Professor Warmdockler is not going to be your First Choice. You never liked the old fart, anyway. On the other hand, you definitely had the hots for the lovely Professor Ziegler, whom you can easily intercept between classes since you memorized her daily schedule last semester.

YOU

Professor Ziegler!

PROF Z

Yes?

YOU

YOUR NAME HERE, from your—

← Run!

PROF Z

I know who you are.

YOU

Great! I mean I know you must have thousands of students—

PROF Z   ← You idiot

Not too many of them make drunken passes at me at local pubs.

YOU   *← Smooth*

Oh, that! That was just a fraternity initiation thing!
Surely you're not going to hold that against me, are
you?

← She is warming up to you. Plug the recommendation.

PROF Z

If you mean, do I plan to report you to the police,
the answer is no.

YOU

That's terrific! I knew you'd be a good sport about
it. Anyway, I was wondering—

PROF Z   *← This isn't really working*

If you mean can I forget your clumsy, insulting,
infantile, disgusting behavior, the answer is also no.

YOU

Of course not! And neither will I. But I think I
may have learned something from the incident,
and I'm now a much, much better person for it.

PROF Z   *← Time for a graceful exit*

I'm glad to hear that, because there was no room
for you to become any worse a person. What do
you want?

YOU

Oh, nothing really. Just wondering what time it
is, but now I hear the bell tower, so, uh, never
mind. Great running into you again!

OK, so Professor Ziegler loses out as well. They can't all be
winners, can they? What about Professor Mallory? Now there's
a guy with a sense of fun.[2]

---

[2]Alcoholic, but tenured.

And you can usually find him at the race track since he has a bit of a gambling problem.

> YOU
>
> Professor Mallory!

> PROF M
>
> Just a minute!

You wait for the 5th race to run its course.

> PROF M
>
> Damn! How could a horse with the name "Sure Winner" come in last?

> YOU
>
> Beats me. I'd have bet on him.

← *good support*

> PROF M
>
> You're from the college aren't you?

> YOU
>
> I'm in your Theory of Numbers seminar.

> PROF M
>
> Oh, yeah. How are you doing? Keeping up with everything, I hope?

← *Very good sign. He doesn't know you.*

> YOU
>
> I'm doing great! I had an A going into the final grading period.

← *Don't push it*

> PROF M
>
> Good for you! I'm sure with a bit of luck, you'll keep that A. You don't happen to have a twenty you could lend me—there's a promising filly who runs really well on grass going off at four to one in the sixth...

YOU

Just what I wanted to talk to you about. I'd really
like to invest some money in your uh, system here,
I'm talking maybe two hundred dollars, but I need
a good letter of recommendation to help me get a
job to pay back the bank I borrowed the money
from to make the investment, if you follow me.

PROF M

I follow you exactly, my friend. And I'd be happy
to give you an excellent letter of recommendation.
I can see you're someone who has the right stuff to
succeed in whatever you put your mind to, and I'll
certainly say that in my letter. Twenties will be fine.

Well. It looks like Professor Mallory is the one! And all it took
was a little preliminary research.

You may be wondering: where are the other nine ways to find out
who will give you a good letter of recommendation, promised in
the title of this chapter. We remind you that a good letter of recommendation is **greatly exaggerated**. So is the title of this chapter.

SUMMARY FOR STUDENTS

Your professors are obligated to give you a letter of recommendation. They are also very busy. We suggest you write your own
and have them sign it.

SUMMARY FOR PARENTS

Most students get good letters of recommendation by recording
four years of high quality academic achievement, so you'd better
give *your* student at least two hundred dollars in bribe money.

CHAPTER 11:

SURVIVING GRADUATION DAY: YOU ARE THE FUTURE— STOP SLOUCHING

Your college graduation day is a day of contrasting emotions, of saying good-bye to friends you may never see again, of grinding boredom at the graduation speeches, a day of entertaining your buddies and parents while keeping them away from each other as much as possible, of accepting warm congratulations from people who might be relatives, and mostly of having pictures taken, which, no matter how bad you may look, will be on the family wall forever.

Following this schedule can help you go through the motions while allowing you the mind space to experience and possibly even enjoy this wonderful day which is, remember, all in honor of you.

GRADUATION DAY SCHEDULE

7:30–7:45 A.M.   A loud RINGING awakens you—it's your mother on the phone, telling you your family is on its way and will be there in five minutes. You jump out of bed in a cold sweat, frantically search for your cap and gown, realize they're gone!

7:45–11:00 A.M. Step up to the podium to give your graduation speech, but you have nothing prepared—look down and realize you never found your cap and gown, and are naked in front of huge audience. Suddenly, your 11th grade history teacher is yelling at you about a paper you never turned in on the causes of the Civil War. He turns into a monster and sets fire to the stage, while the college president screams, "This is all your fault!" and the sirens of the fire trucks are RINGING louder and louder in your ears—

7:30–7:45 A.M.   The loud RINGING awakens you, and you realize you've been having an anxiety dream caused by the stress of graduation. It's your mother—your family will be there in five minutes. You jump out of bed, frantically search for your cap and gown, realize they're gone! No, wait! They're under your bed! Whew!

7:45–8:30 A.M.   Meet family for breakfast, first photo-op of day. Mother has first cry of the day. You have your first nerve steadier from your hidden flask.

8:30–11:00 A.M.   Meet with your classmates (watch other students get honors cords), line up in alphabetical order.

11:00–12:00 noon   Stand around as sun gets hotter, waiting for ceremony to begin.

12:15–12:45 P.M.   March proudly down the aisle to the strains of "Pomp and Circumstance," huge audience applauds wildly.

12:45–12:46 P.M.   Wonder what "pomp and circumstance" means.

12:46–12:50 P.M.   See president of college for first time in your life, as she steps up to the podium.

12:50–1:20 P.M.   Hear president speak about how personally connected she feels to each and every one of you. Look out into audience, unable to find anyone you know. Wonder if your family is out there somewhere.

1:20–1:30 P.M.   Student speaker bursts into tears in an unintelligible medley of broken phrases, voicecracks, sobs and blubbering.[3] Take another nip from your flask.

1:30–2:30 P.M.   Featured graduation speaker gives speech. Feel briefly inspired by something graduation speaker says, then quickly forget what it was.

2:30–2:45 P.M.   Hope and pray your friends and relatives don't make ridiculous displays and noise when you get your diploma.

---

[3]Note to emotional student graduation speakers: a bit of weeping at the podium does add to the emotional resonance of the occasion, however it's a good idea to at least get in a few actual words before breaking down into incomprehensible bawling. If you are subject to these emotional fluctuations, know that there are **good careers** for people who cry easily. Some countries have professional mourners. We have Reality TV.

2:45–2:50 P.M.   Your name is mispronounced over the loudspeaker, you walk across the stage and receive your diploma, wonder why your friends and relatives didn't make ridiculous displays and noise when you got it.

2:50–3:15 P.M.   Listen as hundreds and hundreds of names you've never heard before are called and wonder where these people have been hiding the last four years. Are you at the right graduation? Ask person next to you if you look sunburned. Person next to you asks if your natural coloring is bright pink.

3:15–3:30 P.M.   As President concludes ceremony, cringe at annual joke about the heat.

3:30–4:00 P.M.   Post-graduation reception, massive photo-op, accept congratulations from professors, friends, family, all asking you what you're going to do now. Think to self, "Must kill next person who asks me that." Sneak in another private moment with your flask.

4:30–5:00 P.M.   Your father realizes, while flipping through the pictures he's taken with the new digital camera he's been showing off all day, that some guy stood up right during that crucial, diploma-receiving two seconds, so half of your graduation picture is of the back of someone's ear covering up most of your face.

6:00–8:00 P.M.   Dinner with family and friends and friends' family at fancy restaurant. More photos, more drinks, some laughs, some tears, you stand to give a toast, but are distracted by a car alarm going off outside, forget what you were going to say, then you look down and realize you're naked, the president of your college jumps out from behind a plant with a crossbow, you reach for your sword, but it's not there, your dentist knocks over a candle and the tablecloth catches fire, and the car alarm is RINGING louder and louder,—

7:30–7:45 A.M.   The loud RINGING awakens you, and you realize you've been having an anxiety dream caused by the stress of graduation. It's your mother—your family will be there in five minutes. You jump out of bed, frantically search for your cap and gown, realize they're gone! No, wait! They're under your bed! Whew!

A Few Final Words of Encouragement

Post these messages to yourself on your bathroom mirror, possibly on the sun visor of your car, or the rear view mirror of your bicycle:

"I am not a bum."

"Most people out there are more incompetent than me."

"Thanks to regular medication, I no longer have violent outbursts."

The "bottom line," as they say in the Real World, is that most people learn *on* the job, not before it. Your four (or five or six) years in college have qualified you to be an on-the-job learner because instead of being a callow youth of 18, you are now a callow youth of 22.

Are you ready?

If you'd rather not answer that, try this one: are you any *less* ready than any of the other nincompoops in the job market?

Section Two

Leaving College— Your Personal Journey Through Hell

CHAPTER 12:

Inspirational Quotes

You could have probably bought a book of inspirational quotes to inspire you on your journey through life, but instead, you bought this book. Now you're beginning to regret that decision. But one of the inspirational quotes you might have been reading is "Regret is the spilled trash can you trip over on the dark stairway of life." So basically, you don't want to regret anything.

But just in case you *were* beginning to regret your choice, we're going to provide a list of better, deeper, more advanced inspirational quotes you can use to prove you are a better person than those dopes who only got the regular, inspirational quotes.

Regular Inspirational Quote	Better, Deeper, More Advanced Inspirational Quote
Today is the first day of the rest of your your life!	Yesterday was also the first day of the rest of your life, but you really screwed it up, so you decided to put it off until tomorrow, which is today, but today isn't working out so well, so maybe you should start the rest of your life tomorrow.
Life is not the destination, but the journey.	All journeys lead to the same destination, and all destinations flow from the same journey, so when you come to a fork in the road, and don't know which path to take, choose the one that leads back to where you started, or one of the other ones.

Dreams come true if you believe in yourself.	If you believe in yourself enough, you don't ever have to find a job.
Find a dream and make your dream come true.	Dreams are a purer vision of our better selves, except for that dream where you're naked on stage taking a Spanish final and suddenly you can only speak Japanese. Don't make that one come true.
Follow your heart wherever it leads.	Listen to your heart, but pay particular attention to your liver, because your heart is a little unreliable sometimes, but your liver will never lie to you. Also, your spleen is pretty trustworthy. But when your kidneys start talking to you, it's time to quit drinking.
Never take no for an answer.	Never take no for an answer, except when the question is something like, "Are you throwing me out of the house?" In that case, no is an acceptable answer, and you should take it.
There's no "I" in "TEAM."	You can't spell "unemployed" without a "BA"
Be yourself!	Be yourself unless this isn't a good option for you like because you're a loser. In that case, you're a lot better off being somebody else. Pick somebody superior to yourself and be that person.

A hint for identifying truly inspirational quotes:

Look at the source. If it's not someone you immediately recognize from Daytime Television, be very skeptical.

INSPIRATIONAL SUMMARY FOR STUDENTS

Anybody who requires inspirational quotes to figure out what to do is in even worse shape than you are.

INSPIRATIONAL SUMMARY FOR PARENTS

We didn't mean *you*. That collection of **Oprah Winfrey's** inspirational quotes you've been raving about is really helpful. Really.

CHAPTER 13:

Prioritizing Your Decision-Making: What is the Meaning of Life, or Where Will I Sleep Tonight?

Congratulations! You've graduated. And if you were unable to find a good place to hide in your dormitory, you are now facing the awesome challenges of the rest of your life!

Kind of intimidating, isn't it? As the questions come flooding in, you will have to sort them out into a logical order of **priorities**. For example, the question, "What is the meaning of life?" while it is an outstanding question, does not have an equal urgency with the question, "Where will I sleep tonight?" So we will assess the following 10 questions according to their Relative Level of Urgency (RLU).

Question	Priority Ranking
What is the meaning of life?	Definitely on the low end (see above)
Where will I sleep tonight?	Definitely on the high end.
Who am I?	Another excellent question, and a bit more personal than the meaning of life question, so higher than that one, but lower than where to sleep tonight.

Question	Priority Ranking
What am I going to do with the rest of my life?	Good, but on the broad side. More specific than "Who am I?" so higher than that one, but still lower than the sleeping question.
What career path is right for me?	Important, but can be put off for now.
What job could I actually get?	Higher than the career path thing.
Is this a just society?	Very low.
What can I do to make the world a better place?	Higher than previous question, but lowish.
Should humans live on land or in the water?	What??!
What am I going to have for lunch?	Very high.
Who should I have lunch with?	High, but lower than what to eat.[4]

Next, we ignore the sudden attack of self-doubt generated by that footnote and proceed as we intended, arranging the questions in proper ranking, top to bottom, according to the analysis we've just performed, giving us the following lineup:

1. What am I going to have for lunch?
2. Who should I have lunch with?
3. Where will I sleep tonight?
4. What job could I actually get?
5. What career path is right for me?
6. What can I do to make the world a better place?
7. Is this a just society?
8. What am I going to do with the rest of my life?
9. Who am I?
10. What is the meaning of life?

---

[4]Of course, if you take a job without first deciding Who You Are and What is the Meaning of Life, you may make the wrong decision, and then spend the rest of your life trying to justify it, which would certainly be a **major catastrophe**, so it might be better to prioritize the list from bottom to top. Or maybe you want to start in the middle and expand outwardly in alternating sequence.

Now that you have prioritized these important questions, you can free yourself from the paralysis that can set in when you confront them all at the same time. So take #1 and tackle it! There's McDonald's of course, and that Italian place, and you could eat Chinese, or maybe the deli . . . take as much time as you need, and consult with your friends.

OK! You've made your choice! Good job! That's one question answered! Strike it off the list and go have a well-deserved lunch!

Now you may think that having answered only *one* of these important questions is not a great accomplishment, but according to the latest study, a *vast majority*, 78.4% (plus or minus a sampling error of 42%), of all Americans never get past question number four (What job could I actually get?) in their *entire lives!* So you've really done a lot already!

WAIT A MINUTE

You didn't choose McDonalds, did you? You mean you could have had Chinese, and you chose those cardboard patties and heart-destroying French fries??

What a lousy decision!

Maybe you're not up to this right now. Maybe it would be better to **put off** the decision-making for a while, lest you make a really irreversible **blunder**. It's one thing to have a bad lunch, but you definitely don't want the wrong career, or the wrong marriage, or the wrong meaning of life!

SUMMARY FOR STUDENTS

You should probably just wait, and not rush into any decisions for a while.

SUMMARY FOR PARENTS

Unfortunately, you've already made your lousy decisions, and it's too late to do anything about them now. On the bright side, your really **big mistakes** are mostly behind you, and whatever mistakes are ahead are likely to be smaller ones.

CHAPTER 14:

Navigating and Guiding Your Family Discussions About What You Will Do After College, Including Good Answers to the Big Question— Truthful and Otherwise

Being able to fake an answer to, "So what are you going to do now?" may be **the single most important step** you will take to actually coming up with a *real* answer. The fact that your "provisional" answer may be entirely unrelated to the truth is beside the point. Most people who are bothering you about this subject don't really want to know, and *they will forget almost as soon as you tell them.* They are only asking because they don't want to open a conversation with, "So, have you been doing any interesting drugs?" Or with, "Had any pregnancy scares lately?" So it's always the what-now question.

Good Answers to the Big Question

☺ "I'm planning to go to graduate school in Astrophysics, with the goal of becoming an astronaut, but first I've decided to take a year off to study art in Italy."

Why is this a good answer? Because it puts you on track for a very impressive career, but since you'll be taking a year off first, you don't have to answer any pesky, detailed questions like, "What graduate school are you going to?" Also, since you clearly have a serious and important career in mind, your decision to take a year to study art in Italy becomes **charming** and **well-rounded**, rather than **vague**, **unfocused** and **lazy**.

☺ "I'll be studying the mating habits of orangutans in Borneo, right after I complete my training as a sous chef at *Le Cordon Bleu* in Paris."

☺ "I'm applying for a Fulbright to study dam construction in China, as soon as I finish my internship with the Bolshoi Ballet."

☺ "I'm attempting to be the first person to circumnavigate the earth in a solar-powered catamaran made entirely of bakers' chocolate."

These answers should quiet the casual questioners at a social gathering. However, when dealing with the heightened scrutiny of your own family, you have to be a lot more creative.

We highly recommend that you start these conversations yourself so *you* have taken the initiative and you are **in control**. This not only shows your ambition but may win you flattery points by your earnest appreciation of your parents' wisdom. You will also have seized the element of surprise, a key strategic advantage.

Here are a few suggestions:

WAYS TO INITIATE A CONVERSATION ABOUT YOUR FUTURE

YOU

You know, Dad, I've been thinking about my
future, and I really want to ask your advice, based
on your own life experience.

At this point you can kick back and relax, since your part of the conversation is now **over**. Once in a while it's a good idea to nod your head, and even repeat a phrase or two to give the appearance of close attention, a skill you will have already acquired in college.

Eventually, after a very long time, when your parents have told you the stories of their lives, edited especially for you and embellished with moral and practical lessons, you'll note that the stories have reached the present time, meaning it's time to thank them:

YOU
Wow. That was really helpful. There's so much for me to think about. And I'm going to start right now. Bye.

If your parents beat you to the punch and bring up the subject before you do, you will need a variety of:

Ways to End a Conversation About Your Future

You might be tempted to try: "Don't you want me to be happy?"

Analysis: a dangerous assumption. Your parents may be far more concerned with your ability to buy them a retirement yacht in Florida than your juvenile attachment to happiness. Better to pay close attention to what they are saying and **customize** your response.

The conversation may begin:

PARENT
Have you been thinking about your future?

Analysis: Remember, all in all, this is simply a yes or no question. Therefore, we recommend:

YOU
Yes.

or:

YOU

No.

If you start to ad lib or "wing it" beyond that, your fate is in your own hands.

A more difficult and better thought-out question you may face is:

PARENT

Why aren't you employed?

A simple "yes" or "no" will not suffice. Your strategy here must be more subtle and complex. A crafty way to exit this conversation is the classic answer-a-question-with-a-question technique:

YOU

Why is your shoe untied?

When your parent checks on this unlikely omission, you can seize the opportunity to **run away**.

SUMMARY FOR STUDENTS

Although much of this chapter assumes the opposite, maybe you're someone who is *eager* to be guided by the wisdom and intelligence many years of life experience have given your parents. Maybe you're anxious to repay them for giving you life and nurturing your development by fulfilling *their* dreams for you.

SUMMARY FOR PARENTS

Maybe not.

(Parents still giving you a hard time? We're here to help. Here's another Emergency Chapter from the advanced Careers Section. Next time they ask, tell them you're researching the possibility of a fabulous, well-paying career in jurisprudence, and to prove it, show them (briefly) the following chapter which you are reading.)

CHAPTER 25:

LAW: YOU DON'T HAVE TO BE A LAWYER TO MAKE A LIVING SUING OTHER PEOPLE!

Society is riddled with injustice, unequal treatment, discrimination, corruption, and arbitrary enforcement of the law. The poor and powerless are vulnerable: their concerns are not fairly represented, they don't have access to the best legal defense and they are often run over by laws rather than protected by them. The same is true for our precious wildlife, our beautiful lakes, rivers, streams, and forests, too often plundered and polluted by unscrupulous profiteers.

As you can see, there's plenty of opportunity for a committed individual like yourself to **challenge** these injustices, **fight** for the rights of the downtrodden, and **defend** the unrepresented.

Or you could be a lawyer.

VOCABULARY ALERT

A **lawyer** is a highly trained professional who uses her skill and intelligence to insure that the wealthy and powerful will not be punished for their crimes.

When their clients are celebrities, lawyers also help them sell books and movies based on these misadventures. In the less glamorous area of corporate law, the lawyer quietly helps large corporations avoid paying taxes as well as damages to individuals they have harmed. For example, 43% of all lawyers currently practicing in the United States are engaged in delaying motions on behalf of the **tobacco** industry, in hopes that the plaintiffs will die before they can collect damages. The remaining 57% are engaged in similar litigation on behalf of the automobile industry.

Objection! Aren't there some *good* lawyers out there? What about Clarence Darrow? What about Atticus Finch?

Overruled.

DRAWBACKS TO BEING LAWYER

☹ You will be devoting your time and energy to the gradual destruction of all that is worthwhile in our society by selling your soul to a never-ending parade of the worst, vilest, cruelest, white collar criminals, the rapacious corporations which employ them and their bought-and-paid for henchmen in government, prostituting your talents, education and courtroom skill without regard for truth, fairness or justice, until at last, you'll look at yourself in the mirror one morning and realize your entire life has been one long, agonizing act of capitulation to **Satan**.

PERKS OF BEING A LAWYER

☺ Complimentary membership in some of America's best country clubs.

To find out if you are the type of person naturally well prepared for the challenges of a career in the law, please fill out the following:

LAW APTITUDE QUESTIONNAIRE

When did you first start to think about becoming a lawyer?

Are you sure that was the first time?

How can you be sure?

Couldn't there have been another time before that?

Oh, so now you're not so sure. Now you only *think* that was the first time.

Objection! This isn't a questionnaire! Counsel is badgering the graduate! I make a motion to dismiss this chapter.

Sustained. This entire chapter is completely out of order.

SUMMARY FOR STUDENTS

As long as you always act according to the values and standards you've learned in college, some day you will definitely need a good lawyer.

SUMMARY FOR PARENTS

If your graduate becomes a lawyer, you could save lots of money by getting free legal advice from her, but it would be more prudent to pay someone you could trust.

CHAPTER 15:

NETWORKING (WITH ALL YOUR SLACKER FRIENDS)

→ Developing a rich list of valuable contacts is possibly the most important step to landing that dream job you've always wanted.

"But I don't have any contacts!"

Yes, you do! Go ahead: make a list of everyone you know. Not everyone has to be a CEO. The fact is, everyone on your list knows at least 50 other people. This means that by effectively using your **networking skills,** you could contact almost anyone in the world.

Remember that panhandler outside the liquor store who always hits you up for spare change? This seemingly worthless contact should not be overlooked. In fact, this man has been arrested many times by a police officer who is married to the city attorney, who had an affair with the cable repair guy, who also fixed the cable of Bill Gates' cousin, whose college roommate's father transfers money from an offshore Swiss bank to a financial consultant to the White House, who speaks on a daily basis to the President of the United States of America, who met **Kevin Bacon**!

Now this is a great contact. Kevin Bacon is a *major* celebrity with connections to nearly every major player in show business. Now that you have uncovered this contact, this is the time to catch up with Kevin and see what he can do for you. Write this letter:

Dear Kev,

Long time no see! How's the family? Staying out of trouble? I bet not, ha, ha! I know you're busy, Kev, so I won't waste your time with a lot of chitchat, but I wanted to give you a heads-up that I've grad-

uated now, and I'm looking for a good job. Anything that pays well and is a lot of fun. I figured you know a lot of people, so spread the word that I'm in the market.

Well, I gotta run, but don't be such a stranger, and let me know about those jobs,
Your Name Here

That should work. But while you're waiting for Kevin's friends to call in with those job offers, you can still expand your network.

Now that you have graduated, **everything has changed**. What you called your "address book" in college can become your first "contact list." But considering your new priorities, you have to make some adjustments.

LET'S TAKE ANOTHER LOOK AT YOUR FRIENDS AND RELATIVES

Old Address Book	Current Status	New Contact List
Uncle Joe	Still doesn't have a job.	Get rid of him.
Kid You Disliked in High School	Father owns movie studio, professional sports teams.	In retrospect, not such a bad person after all. Time to renew friendship.
Current Boyfriend/ Girlfriend	Distraction.	Drop.
Your Best Friend	Sleeping on your couch.	Evict.

Now that you have prioritized your relationships, it's time to make your network work for you. But to keep your network contacts interested in helping you, you must offer something to them in return. Of course, you don't want to give them any really good leads. If you had those, you'd use them yourself. What you want to offer are **seemingly** good leads which lead nowhere but leave your networking peers with the feeling they owe you one. Pick out a personalized ad with a name and phone number from the Classifieds (nobody reads them), and offer this person as your inside contact, and the job as a hot lead.

> YOU
>
> Call my friend Andrew—he's one of the top guys at Starbucks. Tell him I recommended you. He's got a couple of hot openings. But keep it hush-hush, this is just for you.

You can give this hot lead to your entire network.
OK. Your network is primed. Time to start making those calls.

WRONG WAY TO MAKE A CALL

> YOU
>
> Hi, Marcie!

> MARCIE
>
> Do I know you?

> YOU
>
> Sure you do! I'm looking for a job. Can you help?

Note how clumsy and **selfish** you appear. But add just a few "extras" and the effect is completely different!

CORRECT WAY TO MAKE A CALL

> YOU
>
> Hi, Marcie!

> MARCIE
>
> Do I know you?

> YOU

Sure you do! We were in the same Remedial Reading class in junior high.

> MARCIE

We were?

> YOU

Uh huh. So how are you doing?

> MARCIE

OK.

> YOU

Fabulous! That's fabulous that you're doing OK. I'm really glad to hear that. How about your family? How are they doing?

> MARCIE

Well, I guess we're all coming to terms with the suicide, if that's what you mean.

> YOU

That's great! You're all coming to terms with the suicide! I'm coming to terms with the fact that I'm looking for new professional opportunities. So I guess we're both coming to terms with something. You don't happen to know about any new professional opportunities which would be appropriate for me, do you?

Note how in the "Correct" version, you don't just blurt out that you want help, but first you establish that you're **sincerely** interested in the person, what they are doing and how their family is getting along. This makes a big difference.

SPECIAL ALERT

If you follow these instructions carefully, you will surely land a job, but that doesn't make your friends and relatives useless. You've invested a lot of time and energy developing your list. You may need it again if you lose your job, and you might even be able to sell it to a telemarketing company. So keep the network alive.

You can express your continuing interest in the individual lives and well-being of each and every contact on your list by sending out a mass mailing of greeting cards during the holiday season. This is a festive time of togetherness, of song and spirit. It is during this season of **giving** that you can most effectively advance your **personal agenda**. You don't have to spend all day on this: a standard template with just a few places to personalize can lighten this task considerably. (See Appendix for sample Individually Customized, Nondenominationally Specific Holiday Networking Card Template.)

So, have you heard from any of Kevin Bacon's friends? Not yet?

SUMMARY FOR STUDENTS

You're *still* hanging out with your best friend? Are you serious about this chapter, or not?

SUMMARY FOR PARENTS

Sorry, but you've been eliminated from your daughter's contact list. Try getting a better job.

CHAPTER 16:

YOUR OWN APARTMENT VS. LIVING AT HOME: COMPARING APPLES AND ORANGES (BOTH OF WHICH ARE ONLY AVAILABLE AT HOME)

Ah! Getting your own place—an exciting first step on the stairway to bankruptcy.

But there are also problems. For example (Fig. 3), the farther away you are from your old dorm, the fewer attractive people your age you will find. Let's take a look:

Fig. 3

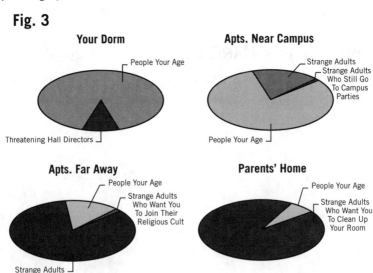

Of course, as an educated person primarily interested in the intellectual attributes of others in your social circle, you personally don't care about how many attractive people your own age are surrounding you at any given time and place, but you have some shallow friends who do care, and *they* need this information.

Advantages of Your Own Apartment
☺ Independence
☺ Learning responsibility
☺ Privacy
☺ Establishing your own identity
☺ Sleep on kitchen floor
☺ Fewer obstacles to becoming full-fledged alcoholic

Disadvantages
☹ Rent.
☹ ♌[5]

Vocabulary Alert
Rent is that amount of money, collected monthly, in advance, given as a bribe to the "landlord" so you won't be **evicted** from your apartment by the **police**.

A **Landlord** is the person who collects this bribe, in exchange for which he promises to fix, but never actually fixes, the many things which are wrong with your apartment, like broken toilets, peeling paint and previous tenants still living in your bedroom.

Ways to Tell if You Have a Good Landlord or a Bad Landlord

Good Landlord (Rare)
☺ "Anything in your apartment need fixing?"

Bad Landlord (Common)
☹ "Where's the rent?"

[5]See Legend, p. 12

Good Landlord (Rare)

☺ "You won't mind if some Calvin Klein models move in next door, will you?"

☺ "I'll be moving to Finland for a couple of years. If you need to fix anything, just deduct it from the rent."

☺ "Will it be all right if I install a Jacuzzi and a big screen TV in your apartment?"

Bad Landlord (Common)

☹ "Where's the rent, Dickhead?"

☹ "Where's the #%!*n' rent, Dickhead?"

☹ "Oh, yeah: there won't be any running water for the next few weeks. And where the hell is the #%!*n' rent, Dickhead?"

This whole, depressing subject is nevertheless one of the *best* reasons you may want to consider living at home, where your parents probably will not charge rent, at least not for the first few months after you return home from college.

CAVEAT[6]

If, when you return, you find a Slovakian family living in your room, your parents are probably already charging rent, and you will not be welcomed by the new tenants. This could create an awkward situation, forcing your parents to choose between you and the Slovakian family, and you may not like how this turns out. But chances are your old room will be waiting for you when you return from college, which means you'll want to consider:

DISADVANTAGES OF LIVING AT HOME

☹ Parents asking pesky questions like:
☹ Why does your room smell like Woodstock?
☹ Are you going out dressed like that?
☹ What you are doing to find a job?
☹ What you are doing?
☹ Who was that young man/woman wandering naked around our house?

---

[6]A Latin word you should have learned by now.

ADVANTAGES OF LIVING AT HOME

☺ No rent.

HELPFUL HINT

While you probably don't want your mother poking around in your room, it's nice to have it cleaned once in a while, but only when you, **not your mother**, wants it cleaned. The best way to accomplish this is to borrow one of those cute little signs you find on doors to hotel rooms, on one side of which is printed in clear, block lettering: DO NOT DISTURB, while on the flip side is the gentle invitation: You May Clean Now (usually with a perky drawing of a maid).

Warning: In order to protect your mother's tender feelings, it's best to take some whiteout and remove the drawing of the maid.

COMPARISON CHART

Pros & Cons of Various Places You May Live After College

	Home	Your Own Apartment	With Roommates	Prison
Cleaning services	Yes ☺	No ☹	No ☹	Yes ☺
People going through your stuff without a search warrant	Yes ☹	No ☺	Maybe ☺	Yes ☹
Meals	Yes ☺	No ☹	No ☹	Yes ☺
Food in refrigerator	Yes ☺	No ☹	Maybe ☺	No ☹
Pesky questions like will you be home for dinner	Yes ☹	No ☺	No ☺	No ☺
Arguments over really dumb stuff	Yes ☹	No ☺	Yes ☹	Yes ☹
Individual liberties	No ☹	Yes ☺	Yes ☺	No ☹
Whuppin' from the Warden	No ☺	No ☺	No ☺	Yes ☹

If you decide that the advantages of living in an apartment outweigh the advantages of living at home, or putting it slightly differently, your parents are driving you crazy, you will want to pick out a suitable apartment building to live in. Many of them have signs out front which can reveal a lot.

GOOD SIGN

☺ "If you are going to nearby bars and clubs, please curtail loud celebrations after 2:00 A.M."

BAD SIGN

☹ "Medicare accepted"

GOOD SIGN

☺ "Singles mixer Saturday night, BYOB"

BAD SIGN

☹ "Sunday is Bingo Night"

REALLY BAD SIGN

☹☹ 19TH AVE. MONSTABOYZ

FURNISHING YOUR APARTMENT

→ Important note: Your parents will be very helpful in offering to give you furniture from the garage or attic to furnish your apartment. Do NOT accept these items. Your parents have been trying to get rid of this stuff for 30 years—they have been unable to sell, or even give them away at garage sales for *decades*. They have called Goodwill and the Salvation Army to pick them up, and neither group has accepted these items.

WHAT YOU WILL NEED

Furnishing an apartment is not done overnight, but you have to start somewhere, which means prioritizing your requirements. You must distinguish between those items you want and those items you need:

Essential	Useful	Luxury
N-64	Mini putting green	Chairs
Tiki bar	Indoor bowling	Bed
Babbling Brook Peace Fountain™	Ten person hookah	Lamps
Bottle opener	Decorative plants	Cups, glasses, silverware
Air hockey table	Pool table	Dining room table[7]

SUB-CHAPTER 16A: SUBLETTING

Subletting is God's gift to unemployed renters. What was a seemingly impossible amount of rent money to come up with can be magically reduced by effective use of your living space.

Say your four bedroom house costs $2000 a month to rent. Your share is $500. However, by opening your living space to a few more friends, your monthly rent can be made a lot more affordable, as shown in Fig. 4:

---

[7]This might be a good time to acknowledge the gender bias in this chapter, and perhaps one or two others. It's not that we're insensitive, it's just that we don't know what women want in their apartments. Maybe some nice soaps?

Fig. 4

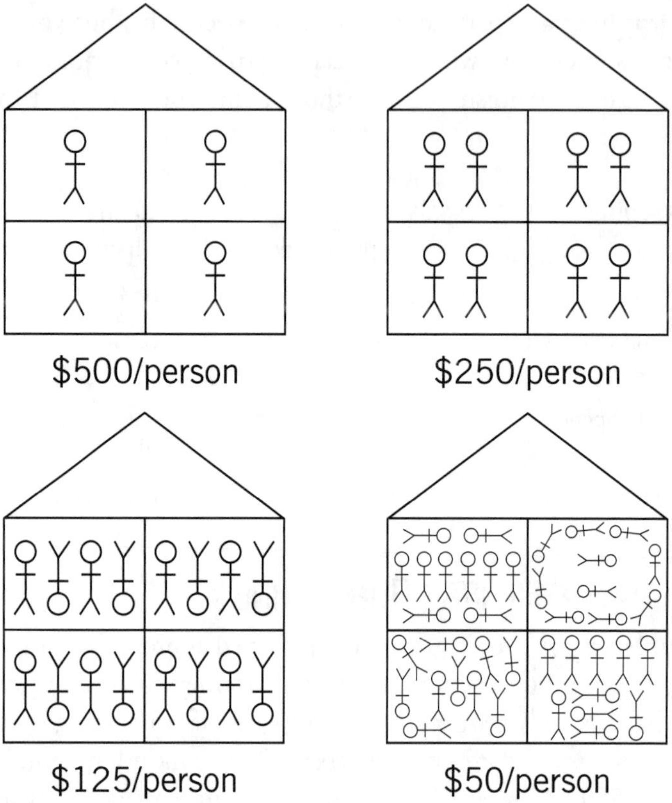

$500/person

$250/person

$125/person

$50/person

There! You can afford 50 bucks, can't you? But you may think so many people would not fit comfortably into one room. Not so. By using room dividers creatively (as shown in Fig. 5), an average bedroom can easily accommodate whatever number of rent payers you need. You can attract these potential rent payers by the way in which you describe your living space, not unlike the way Bed and Breakfast Inns describe their rooms. And since you probably haven't gotten around to cleaning up those Cheez-Its you spilled a couple of months ago, your place really *is* kind of a Bed and Breakfast.

Fig. 5

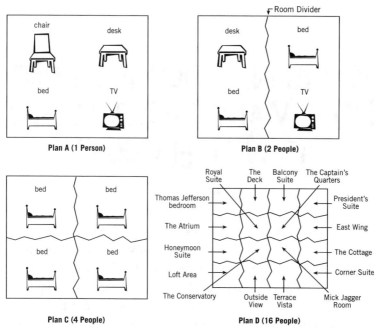

Plan A (1 Person)

Plan B (2 People)

Plan C (4 People)

Plan D (16 People)

SUMMARY FOR STUDENTS

Just because it's your own apartment and you can do whatever you want, you don't *have* to become a full-fledged alcoholic and sleep on the kitchen floor. You can sleep in the bathtub.

SUMMARY FOR PARENTS

That couch you generously gave your kid to help furnish her apartment was really quite lovely and it's been *very* useful. There is no truth whatsoever to the rumor that she tossed it over a cliff in the dead of night. She took it to the city dump in the middle of the day, paid the fee, and disposed of it properly.

CHAPTER 17:

Managing Your Finances: How Many Credit Cards is Not Enough?

Now that you've graduated, it's time to take control of your finances. In the real world you must earn your keep by the sweat of your own brow, and more importantly, learn the habits of **thrift** and **responsibility**. By careful planning, drawing up a budget and sticking to it, keeping detailed accounts of every financial transaction, balancing your checkbook and scrutinizing every bill, you can learn to live within your means.

Or you could put everything on a credit card.

Vocabulary Alert

A **credit card** is a magical device invented by altruists with your **best interests** in mind, to bridge the gap between what you want and what you can afford. It's something like a research stipend or a grant. If you're lucky enough to have been selected to receive a credit card, take it! Consider it a compliment—someone has been viewing your many accomplishments with respect, and considers you worthy. You must have done something special— congratulations!

Another piece of magic: when the monthly statement arrives, you'll notice that you don't have to pay the entire amount—only a small **portion** of it! If you get this deal, it's another achievement for you. It means the bank has faith in you and wants to help you achieve your **ultimate goals**!

Vocabulary Alert

Interest is when someone from the bank takes a special notice, or fancy, to the work you've been doing with their money. Sometimes, if you're a very special person, the bank will take a very large **amount** of interest in you!

Saving Money

It can be difficult for a young person, living in the moment, to grasp the importance of putting money away for the future. But the following comparison chart will give you an insight into the advantages of saving.

Things You Could Spend Your Money On Now	Things You Could Spend It On Later
Drum set	Your ungrateful children
Surf board	Taxes
Trip to Hawaii	College tuition fund
Dune buggy	Electric powered wheelchair
Huge party	Pre-need burial trust fund
Tequila collection	Liver transplant

Now that you fully appreciate the importance of planning for your future, you're ready for:

12 Simple Steps To Financial Independence

1. Draw up a list of your personal financial goals. Where do you want to be five years from now? Where do you want to be ten years from now?
2. Determine a percentage of your monthly income to contribute to a 401k plan, appropriate to your financial goals.
3. Obtain a credit card with a reputable company.
4. Pay off first credit card by obtaining another credit card. Pay off the second credit card with a third card, and if necessary, the third with a fourth.

5. Declare bankruptcy, start afresh.
6. Change your name.
7. Move to another state. (Not just another city, you must actually cross the state line.)
8. Change your appearance. Cut hair, grow beard (men), change hair color (women).
9. Obtain fake ID's.
10. Put whatever money you've borrowed into a numbered Swiss bank account.
11. Change appearance even more with plastic surgery.
12. Learn foreign language, move to a country which has no extradition treaty with the U.S.[8]

INSURANCE

Aw jeez, do we really have to get into details about everything? No—you've done a lot already this week, and darned if this isn't about the most boring subject in the world. Health, dental, fire, car, life, blah, blah. It's gotta be the last thing on your mind right now, huh? Look: don't crash your car, brush your teeth. You'll be fine. Take the rest of this chapter off and go rest up. Have a drink or two and go for a drive.

SUMMARY FOR STUDENTS

Now that you know so much, you could become a financial consultant. Telling people how to manage their money might be the best way to get yourself out of debt.

SUMMARY FOR PARENTS

Speaking of debt, now that your student is through with college and it's time to pay off that college tuition loan, you might want to familiarize yourself with the list of countries with no extradition treaties with the United States (see footnote).

---

[8]Barbados, Brazil, Cambodia, China, Costa Rica, Cuba, Dominica, El Salvador, Ethiopia, Haiti, Honduras, Indonesia, Iran, Ireland, Jordan, Laos, Libya, Malawi, Malaysia, Maldives, Nigeria, Pakistan, Panama, Paraguay, Russia, Saudi Arabia, Switzerland, Syria, Taiwan, Ukraine, and Vanuatu, if you must know.

CHAPTER 18:

A WORD ABOUT PETS (AVOID)

This period of your life is extremely fluid, in that you do not know where you will be or what you will be doing as you look ahead to, for example, tomorrow.

Therefore, you do NOT want to acquire a pet. Of course you already know this, but what you may not know is that making a conscious decision to acquire a pet is the **least common way** of getting one.

To avoid the more common ways of acquiring a pet:

Do NOT agree to "watch" a pet for anybody else for ANY length of time, including "for **five minutes** while I run down to the market." Those 10 words happen to be the most common introduction to **lifetime ownership** of an unwanted pet.

The second most common way of acquiring a pet is getting romantically and/or sexually involved with someone who has one. Use EXTREME caution in forming any kind of **attachment** to someone with a pet. Our advice is total AVOIDANCE, but sometimes true love makes this **impossible**. Therefore, pay close attention to:

WHAT TO DO IF YOU RETURN TO YOUR APARTMENT AND FIND THE FOLLOWING CODED NOTE

Dear John,
Suddenly called away for the weekend to Hong Kong on business. Please feed Frufru in the morning (dog food is on the counter), and

walk her once in the afternoon and once at night (poopoo baggies also on counter).
Thanks!
Love you to death,
Marcie

TRANSLATION

Dear John,
I've decided to dump you, and also to dump Frufru. You are both holding me back, and neither of you is totally house trained.
You will never hear from me again,
Marcie

If you read a note like this, put it back down on the table gently, then back away SLOWLY, exit the residence at once, NOT stopping to take anything with you, and never return, ever. You may want to call an animal rescue organization, the kind that will not euthanize Frufru. (Then again, depending on your relationship with the pet, you may just want to call the pound.)

GOOD NEWS ABOUT PETS

What if (just hear us out for a second) Frufru turns out to have some talent and can be in a dog show or in the circus or on **TV**? ☺ Maybe she is worth something after all. You could live vicariously through your dog who has the exciting career you were never able to find.

BAD NEWS

☹ It can be damaging to your self-esteem to be outdone by your dog. Plus, your dog will have new, cooler friends in Show Biz and won't want to hang out with you anymore.

A WORD ABOUT PETS, PART II: BABIES

In addition to pets, another pitfall of intergender relationships is babies. Unless you are quite sure you want one, having a baby is **not recommended**, particularly in cases where the relationship has not yet passed the all important 48-hour mark. But if you have a strong need to nurture, you should study the following pet/baby comparison chart:

	Your Pet	Your Baby
Ease of Feeding	☺ Pretty easy	☹ Applesauce in your eye
Medical Help Availability	☺ Vet—good	☺ Pediatrician—good except when ☹ baby is sick
Sleep Issues	☺ Good—pets sleep a lot	☹ Bad—*you* will never sleep again
Unwanted Advice	☹ Everyone is an expert	☹ Your parents will stop criticizing your parenting when they are dead, if you're lucky

In general, babies are a lot of work for the first six months, but eventually they'll become your first employee.

SUMMARY FOR STUDENTS

If you somehow acquire pets or children, you can always palm them off on your parents.

SUMMARY FOR PARENTS

If your offspring acquire pets or children, move to another country.

CHAPTER 19:

You Don't Have Time to Read This Chapter

If you're still in college, time is running out! There's so much to do before you graduate, and so little time!

If you've already graduated, you've discovered that life in college was really a cakewalk—you were taken care of by a squadron of angels who looked after your every need. In the real world you have to take care of your needs by yourself, and do a whole lot more besides. Moreover, right now, while you're reading this, there's another college graduate just like you, only with better abs and a stricter regimen of dental hygiene, who is out stealing the good job you should be looking for. ☹ You **definitely** don't have time for this chapter.

Therefore, you may be excused from reading it. But,

☺☺☺☺☺☺ you *will* be given credit for it, ☺☺☺☺☺☺

because this is such a caring book.

Special Note for Parents

You have been so busy for so long, the moment you saw you didn't have time for this chapter you immediately moved on to the next one, or possibly the one after that, so you aren't even reading this. And if you're not going to bother to read this note, we're certainly not going to bother to write it, even though it might have contained something very valuable.

CHAPTER 20:

Navigating and Guiding Your Family Discussions About What Your Child Will Do After College— A Study Guide for Parents (Students: Skip This at Your Own Risk)

Good News for Students

☺ You can skip this chapter completely!

Bad News for Students

☹ We suggest you *not* skip this chapter, or you'll be easy pickin's for wised-up parents.

Can it be that your little child, the one who just yesterday, it seems, was taking her first, shaky steps across the living room floor while learning to pronounce words like "Momma" and "Dada," is now taking her first, shaky steps across the graduation stage, while learning to pronounce words like "debt consolidation" and "unemployed"?

It is a time of mixed feelings for everyone, and for parents especially, combining your anxiety about your child's future with the tearful pride which comes from knowing your child has successfully met the intellectual challenge of four years of higher education, emerging as a capable, informed, confident young adult, and that you will **no longer be paying for college!**

Which brings us to the first important subject: Graduate School.

IMPORTANT ADVICE

In today's complex, competitive world, an advanced degree is increasingly valuable. Even though it is expensive, you must let your child know that if she wants to continue on for a Masters or a Ph.D., you will be proud and honored to make any sacrifice to finance this crucial investment in her future.

MORE IMPORTANT ADVICE

There is an optimum time to tell her this—that time is one day after the graduate schools have stopped accepting applications for next year. Then tell her how common it is for students to apply to graduate schools after taking some time off after college. Don't worry—by the time applications are being accepted next year, she will have destroyed so many brain cells drinking, no grad school in their right mind will accept her!

So: with any luck, your kid won't be going to graduate school. But that leaves the future still an open question, and the answer is going to be of keen interest to you parents, because you want the best for your child, and also because if she doesn't come up with a good answer pretty soon, she will be back home again, eating your food.

OPENING GAMBITS FOR THE CONVERSATION ABOUT YOUR CHILD'S FUTURE

As noted in previous chapters, there will be more than enough adults among your friends and relatives, not to mention perfect strangers, who will be bombarding your student during her senior year with the "What are you gonna do now?" question. There is no need for *you* to join this dismal choir! Instead, in order to gently guide the conversation into this delicate area, we suggest:

"Gosh! I was just reading about how there are so many wonderful opportunities for college graduates these days! If *I* was graduating from college right now, I think I'd be so overwhelmed by all these great possibilities, I wouldn't know *what* to do!"

OK—maybe that's not the greatest opening gambit. But you have to start somewhere. If you can't think of anything else, try one of these:

"Say, can I borrow 50 bucks until next Tuesday? Oh, I forgot! You don't have a job. Never mind, I'll go down to the corner and hold up the liquor store."

"I just ran into Sarah McGillicutty. She told me Karen just graduated from college and already has a great job, and she's deaf, dumb and blind."

"Did you hear about Josh Squire? He graduated six months ago, couldn't find a job, just moped around the house until one day he took a shotgun down to the mall. They had to call the SWAT team, and he died in a hail of machine gun fire. Such a nice boy, too."

"Your alumni association just called. They wanted to know what you're doing. What should I tell them?"

You'll note that all the above gambits include at least one of the Three Great Motivators: **Fear**, **Shame**, and **Guilt**. As long as you stick with these, you can be as creative as you like.

In general, a good strategy for having a successful discussion about your child's future is to **lock** all the **doors** and **windows** first. That way, she can't escape.

USING YOUR LOUSY CONNECTIONS TO HELP YOUR GRADUATE

Your headstrong kid may absolutely refuse your help, insisting naively on doing everything "by herself" in spite of your constant offers to use your connections on her behalf. In this case, you're off the hook! Whatever happens from here on out is her fault, not yours. It's not like you didn't try. But maybe your kid will eventually allow you to "help." This means you're going to have to ask your friends and/or business and professional connections for a favor, sometimes referred to as "calling in your chits." Here is a sample dialogue you might have with your graduate about this situation:

> YOU
> I spoke to Bill Richards about you today—

> YOUR GRADUATE
> Bill Richards!? You mean that totally creepy pervert who tried to hit on me when I baby sat for his kids when I was in high school??!! I wouldn't work for him if he was the last man on earth!

> YOU
> (offended)
> Well, if you're going to be picky....

Note that you are now **off the hook again.** You did what you could—in fact, you went way out on a limb for her, and ungrateful wretch that she is, she spurned your best efforts.

SUMMARY FOR STUDENTS

Remember, your parents know more than anyone about what *they* should have done after college. They don't actually know anything about what you should do. Anyway, why would you take advice from someone who thinks "Women's Studies" (your major) is the study of cooking and cleaning?

SUMMARY FOR PARENTS

"Women's Studies" is no longer *just* about cooking and cleaning. Better keep up.

(The dog ate Chapter 21.)

CHAPTER 22:

A TOURIST'S GUIDE TO THE REAL WORLD: KNOWING HOW YOU'RE DOING WITHOUT GRADES

Since you've been away for four (or five or six) years, you've probably forgotten about some of the quaint customs and idiomatic expressions used by natives of what is called "The Real World."

CATCH PHRASES YOU WILL NEED

"Please"—this signifies a polite desire for a given result.

Thus, the college phrase, "Gimme that," becomes, in the Real World, "Please gimme that."

"Thank you"—this is a phrase used to conclude an exchange in which a desired result has been achieved.

Thus, if you've been given whatever it is you asked for when you said, "Please gimme that," instead of (college) "Yeah," you say, (Real World) "Thank you."

College Expression	Real World Equivalent
My grandmother died, I need an extension.	My grandmother died, I'll get it to you on Monday.
The dog ate my term paper.	The dog ate my resume.
(Lift your chin one inch.)	I'm pleased to meet you.

Quaint Customs

Most Real World natives get out of bed each morning at about the same time.

Warning: it's quite early!

Also: they tend to go to bed each night at the same time—also quite early, often before midnight!

This odd schedule is designed primarily to accommodate another bizarre custom of the Real World called "work."

Vocabulary Alert

Work 1. That activity which your whole life up to now has been preparing you to accept which makes you a mindless cog in the machinery oppressing and enslaving the vast majority of humanity so that somebody you don't even know and can't imagine will have an Olympic size swimming pool and a shuffleboard court in their second vacation home, while you gradually surrender every ounce of your creativity and independence to amass a retirement savings account which will eventually be stolen by the man with the shuffleboard court. 2. That activity which can be exchanged for "money," which can then be exchanged for food, clothing, shelter, and if there's any left after that, movie rentals.

Fun Facts

The Real World is filled with people a lot **younger** than you, and also a lot **older** than you! Some of these people are known as "children." Others are known as "Old People" or "Senior Citizens."

Warning: *Neither* of these groups are into the same music you are into. They have never heard of the bands you like, so you may as well just forget about communicating with them on a serious level. Nonetheless, you may be **required** to converse with them on a superficial level, and you should be prepared to do this.

SUBJECTS NOT RECOMMENDED

1) politics
2) religion
3) body art

SUBJECTS RECOMMENDED

1) today's weather
2) food (possibly)
3) tomorrow's weather

There are other important **differences** between your life in college, and your life after college.

Life in College	Life After College
Coed dorms	Lousy apartments
Lots of not-so-great food you don't pay for	Lots of not-so-great food you do pay for
Sympathetic friends who secretly want your girlfriend or boyfriend	Sympathetic friends who secretly want your job
Somewhat suspicious campus cops	Extremely suspicious real cops
Idiots passing arbitrary judgments on you	Idiots passing arbitrary judgments on you

Unlike in college, Real World humans are only allowed to eat certain foods. Fortunately, you can still get the same nutrients you got in your old diet in socially acceptable Real World food:

College Diet	Provides	Real World Diet
Fried Twinkie	Starches	Baked Potato
Vending Machine	Sugars	Apple
40's of King Cobra	Personality	Cabernet '82
Methamphetamines	Cardiovascular Exercise	Starbucks

SUMMARY FOR STUDENTS

In the real world Starbucks isn't the only way to get cardiovascular exercise. Though it requires significantly more time, effort and self-discipline, you can also brew your own coffee at home.

SUMMARY FOR PARENTS

For *your* cardiovascular exercise, we suggest you buy a comfortable pair of running shoes, block out at least a half an hour in your daily schedule, and stick your finger in an electrical socket.

CHOOSING A CAREER BY PROCESS OF ELIMINATION

CAREER ELIMINATION EXERCISE

So many careers, so little time. But which one to choose? One method is the process of elimination. Here's how it works: We pose a few simple, multiple choice questions (you should be pretty good at those by now), you answer them, and according to your answers you either list the career as a definite possibility, or cross it off your list. Ready?

1. How important to you are your teeth?
A) Pretty attached to all of them
B) Really like the ones in front
C) Can whistle better without 'em
If you answered A) or B), the career of **Professional Hockey Player** is not for you. Cross that one off your list, and proceed to:

2. How important to you is the truth?
A) I cannot tell a lie
B) I'd rather not lie
C) I live to lie
If you answered A) or B), the career of **Presidential Press Secretary** is out. Eliminate that one and don't ever look back. Proceed to:

3. Financial security is
A) Very important
B) Important, but not as important as happiness
C) Insignificant

If you even bothered to answer this question, the career of **Professional Actor** is not for you. Proceed as quickly as possible to:

4. My concentration is excellent, but it can occasionally be broken by
A) Sexual fantasies
B) Annoying insects
C) Major earthquakes
If your concentration can be broken by *anything*, please don't become an **Air Traffic Controller**, OK? It will be a big relief to the rest of us. Just proceed to:

5. How big a part of your morning is alcohol?
A) Pretty big part
B) Usually add it to orange juice
C) Never get up without it
If you answered A), B), or C), the career of **Neurosurgeon** is not for you, but you should really consider being a **Presidential Press Secretary**.

CHAPTER 23:

THE MILITARY: GETTING ACCEPTED INTO THE MILITARY SERVICES IS NOT THAT DIFFICULT!

As recently as just a few years ago college grads generally did not consider a military career, but today, with **new challenges** facing our country and a new surge of patriotism sweeping the land, this option is being considered once again, especially by those with absolutely **no clue** about what else to do.

Warning: Former officers Tom Cruise, Tom Hanks, Richard Gere, Jack Nicholson, Gene Hackman, Denzell Washington and Demi Moore are no longer in the military. Also: Kelly McGillis will NOT be your flight instructor.

DO I QUALIFY?

Getting accepted into the military services is not that difficult! Here are a few questions to ask yourself to see if you meet the requirements:

Can you walk? Never mind! Can you breathe?

Forget breathing: do you have a more or less steady pulse? If so, you're in!

Of course a high school diploma (you have one of those, don't you?) is generally preferred, but lack of one may not prevent you from a career in the military, especially during times of **national**

emergency, loosely defined as whenever the recruiter is having trouble meeting the monthly quota, which is all of the time.

Also, while more than a couple of **felony** convictions, or, in military parlance, "youthful mistakes" on your record is frowned upon, during times of national emergency (see above) this can be **overlooked**.

OTHER ADVANTAGES OF A MILITARY CAREER

After many years cooped up in small classrooms under the thumb of **capricious teachers** enforcing arbitrary rules, young men and women will be eager to enter a vigorous outdoor life where they will be driven through muddy fields by **capricious drill instructors** enforcing arbitrary rules. But more than this, an active, physical life of challenge will sculpt their flabby, civilian bodies into toughened hunks of martial muscle, and their flabby, civilian minds into toughened hunks of martial muscle.

Also, as anyone who has seen their fast-paced TV ads can confirm, the military services offer adventure, excitement, challenge, travel, new and useful skills, leadership training, pride, patriotism, belonging, and really **ugly haircuts**.

Alert for women: the guys-to-girls ratio in the military is *very* favorable. You will have your pick of tens of thousands of men who cried at the end of *Gladiator*. (Note: Russell Crowe is also no longer in the military. Neither is Mel Gibson. They are both doing expert military analysis and commentary on Fox News.)

DISADVANTAGES OF A MILITARY CAREER

There are only a couple of disadvantages of a military career, which isn't a lot considering the many advantages mentioned above.

1) Most of your peers will be people who barely made it out of high school.
2) You could be killed.

GOOD NEWS

☺ While it's true you could be killed, ours is the biggest and best military in the world, and as a member of the United States Armed Forces you will be the best trained and equipped fighting man or woman on earth. This means that although you cannot rule out the possibility that you could be killed by an enemy soldier, you are a hell of a lot more likely to be killed by "**friendly fire**" from one of your own comrades.[9]

BAD NEWS

☹ You will be just as dead. In fact, given the high degree of skill and superior fire power of the U.S. Military forces, you will probably be somewhat deader. But there is no malice connected with friendly fire, only the best of intentions and friendliest of feelings. Also, you will have died for your country and will have the eternal gratitude of your fellow citizens, and somebody in your family gets a nice flag.

HOW YOUR MAJOR MATCHES UP WITH FUTURE POSITIONS IN THE MILITARY

Your Major	Roles in the Military
Math	Shooting People with Guns
Physics	Shooting People with Bigger Guns
Communications	Propaganda & Disinformation Officer
Creative Writing	Making Up Those Cute Names for Invasions Like "Operation Shooting People with Guns"
International Law	N/A

---

[9]It is a violation of the Military Code of Conduct for the Army, Navy, Air Force and Marines to share a common radio frequency. While this sometimes leads to "friendly fire" casualties because they can't talk to each other, it guarantees the security of each branch of the armed services in the event that any one of them declares war on the others.

SUMMARY FOR STUDENTS

We certainly need a strong military, today more than ever! In order to maintain a strong military, young people like yourself must volunteer to serve and protect their country. (Note: An alert person such as yourself will read the previous sentence carefully and realize that it says, "...young people *like* yourself must volunteer to serve and protect their country." This does *not* mean that you, personally, must volunteer, only that someone *like* you must volunteer.)

SUMMARY FOR PARENTS

If your son is a disobedient, undisciplined, potentially dangerous sociopath, there is no better institution than the United States Military to transform him into an obedient, disciplined definitely dangerous sociopath.

CHAPTER 24:

FABULOUS CAREERS, OR CAREERS IN FABULOUSNESS

What could be more **fabulous** than a career in design? There's interior design, body sculpting, and the most fabulous of all, fashion design.

"But I'm a college student," you cry. "I've spent my last four years in rags. I don't know anything about design!"

Au contraire, as we in the fashion business like to say. Wearing rags is the best qualification on earth to become a **Fashion Designer**. All you need now is a bunch of fabulously beautiful, anorexic fashion models to wear your rags. Find these people (they're the ones with long limbs, long necks, thick lips, high cheekbones and no discernible waistlines), make sure they aren't fed more than the absolute minimum needed to maintain life, rip up some cloth (not too much), and throw them on the models. This is your "collection."

If the models are beautiful enough, your **collection** will be greeted with wild applause, and the **buyers** will buy it for their stores. The buyers are already in a pretty good mood, since high fashion shows are usually held in fabulous places like **Paris**, France, and **Milan**, Italy, and the buyers' trips have been **paid for** by their employers. Same with the writers and photographers with the fashion magazines. As long as you keep your actual clothing to a minimum, revealing as much of the beautiful models' beautiful bodies as possible, your collection will be anointed as "**bold**" and "**fresh**," the two key words in the fashion industry.

Soon, eager customers will be buying your clothes at fabulous prices in clothing stores. They will see the models wearing these clothes, and conclude, **logically** enough, that if they buy these clothes, they will look like those models. By the time they actually put them on and take a long look at themselves in the mirror, you will be long gone, or as we say in the fashion business, *"au revoir longtemps."*

At this point, another set of designers takes over, the ones who design **Fitness Clubs**. The customer with your rags has come to the shocking realization that she lacks a certain *je ne sais quoi* which the models have, and it may be related to the relative fitness of the customer as opposed to the models. So the customer now seeks information in the same, reliable place she has used to get information about what clothes to buy: the advertising pages of newspapers and magazines, where she discovers that all the people who are pictured at the local fitness club have fabulous bodies, which means that all she needs to do is join up.

In the **good old days**, people didn't need these clubs. They stayed fit by working hard at physical labor all day long, and died an early death due to **overwork**. But they were very fit. In the Post-Industrial Age, machines do a lot of the hard physical labor, with the result that most Americans are now, not to mince words, **fat**. But thanks to the Health and Fitness Industry, we now have elaborate, expensive machines to help us exercise, along with expensive powders and potions, available exclusively at the clubs, to increase our fitness. After just a few months' committed effort at the club, the customer discovers that the people featured in the ads in the newspapers, magazines and TV, were, in fact, also **models**, and that she still doesn't look like any of them in the mirror, wearing your rags. So she turns to the next design professional, the Personal Trainer.

The **Personal Trainer** is a highly trained individual who is certified by a professional organization to which the personal trainer pays a fee to get a certificate which says he or she is a

→ Certified Personal Trainer ←

If you happen to have the money to pay this fee, this could be you. The Personal Trainer then gives the client a five page questionnaire with detailed questions about the client's day-to-day routine, including times of waking and sleeping, resting heart rate, personal eating habits, natural activity level and overall health. The Trainer then takes this information, and disappears into the Data Processing Office of the Health Club. After making the client wait for at least 20 minutes, the Trainer emerges with an

Individually Customized Personal Health and Fitness Program

which reads:

Exercise More and Eat Less.

Then the Personal Trainer collects a handsome fee, which more than makes up for the cost of buying the certificate.

But alas, sooner or later the customer will again stand (if all that work with the complicated fitness machines has not resulted in a permanent injury which prevents standing), in front of the mirror in your rags, and will **still** not look like that model. So it's time to call in the cosmetic surgeons, yet another branch of the great design industry.

It is the job of the **Cosmetic Surgeon** to make an aging, not-so-beautiful person with too much money look young and beautiful. This works wonderfully well, except in the majority of cases in which the aging, not-so-beautiful person ends up looking like an aging, not-so-beautiful person who has had cosmetic surgery.

By this time, the rags you originally designed are way out of fashion, and even if the customer looked like the original, fabulously beautiful, anorexic high fashion model, the clothes are *so* yesterday. The customer must face the fact that in order to be fabulous, she will have to settle for living in a fabulous home. Now it's time for the **Interior Designer**.

It is the job of the Interior Designer to design a living environment for the person with way too much money and no idea how to be fabulous. Just how fabulous the customer can be will depend on how much money they have. The basic amount of money, of course, is the Interior Designer's fee. Once that is covered, the degree of fabulousness will depend on, for example, if the customer has enough money to go for the brushed Italian marble countertop, or something a bit more *déclassé*, whatever that means. The well-trained Interior Designer is always sensitive to the inevitable **compromises** which a budget of some kind demands, even if the solid gold plumbing fixtures which would add so much to the master bathroom must be copper instead. However, just a slight grimace and perhaps a raised eyebrow here and there will convey the important message that if the customer insists on being cheap, it is not the fault of the Interior Designer when the ultimate result is a lifestyle less fabulous than it might have been.

SUMMARY FOR STUDENTS

The great thing about design is that you get to design fabulous clothes which you don't actually have to wear, and fabulous living environments which you don't actually have to live in.

SUMMARY FOR PARENTS

As you get older, the greatest design innovation you can make in your own environment is to gradually decrease the number of, and finally eliminate, mirrors.

CHAPTER 26:

Careers in Computers: Fatal Error E06#58647 Has Occurred

Good News

☺ Graduating with a degree in Computer Science, you're a tremendously desirable potential employee, on the **cutting edge** of tomorrow's technology. You'll be starting out with a huge advantage over almost every other classmate, an advantage you can leverage into a rewarding and satisfying career almost immediately.

Bad News

☹ A 6th grader can work computers way better than you without even trying.

Good News

☺ If the 6th grader makes fun of you, you can still kick his ass up and down the playground.

Bad News

☹ If you do this, he will hack into your computer and **blow up** your house.

Looking On the Bright Side

☺ Your house wasn't really worth nearly as much as you thought it was.

MORE GOOD NEWS

☺ As a college graduate with a background in computers, you qualify for a fabulous job at a startup company, launched just a year ago in somebody's **garage**, but it's now quite successful, and you'll still be getting in on the ground floor, creating as you go, with young, exciting coworkers, a totally **casual** work environment where you don't have to wear a coat and tie, people respect your work, the challenges are really interesting, and you get all kinds of **stock options** along with full benefits and a great starting salary!

MORE BAD NEWS

☹ That company just went **out of business**.

OK. So you're having a little trouble finding that second job. No problem, we're here to help.

To be employable in the computer world, you must have the latest software upgrades, which you don't have. But you can upgrade your computer by yourself at home. So let's get started:

Take out that old computer of yours and delete the following: All devices listed in the Device Manager in the Other Devices category, all entries under config.sys, and everything in the **cache**. Have you done that? Good. Now open the Hard Disk Controller and remove any usb drive. Now go to the Universal Serial Bus Controller category and remove any entry with a red X, or a yellow! If either the **Root Hub** or the Controller is duplicated, remove all entries. Now **reboot** your system. Ignore the warning message, just do it.

OK, if your computer just froze, or you can't get online anymore, you'll have to go to the online Tech Help site.

No, *of course* you can't go to the Online Tech Help site on the computer which is frozen or can't get online. Calm down. Use your **backup** computer.

Why didn't you tell us you don't have a backup computer? Well, never mind, just call Tech Help.

We're sorry, but all of our technical support operators are busy.

Wait. There's Good News: ☺ your computer has just come up on our **remote server**.

There's also some Bad News: ☹ your computer has been infected with a sophisticated **virus**, thoroughly hacked by teenagers operating from Moscow, and the Russian **mafia** now has access to your **bank account**.

And your computer just crashed.

Oh! And it just caught **fire**. You'd better delete your internet browser now, and also get out of the house, taking all pets with you.

Maybe this just isn't the right field for you.

Upgrade this advice now—ignore previous paragraph, it's now obsolete, and no longer compatible with the current paragraph. The Device Driver for the last sentence will not work on the next sentence. Get new Driver now.

VOCABULARY ALERT

A **Macintosh** is a computer which has no problems whatsoever, unless you buy one.

A **program** is a complex series of computer instructions which only works on a PC, unless you own a PC, in which case it only works on a Macintosh (see above).

SUMMARY FOR STUDENTS

If there is a problem with the advice you just got, it's **not our fault**. You have to talk to the editor or the bookseller, who will refer you to the distributor or the publisher, who are not available.

SUMMARY FOR PARENTS

Computers are typewriters designed only for experts and children. They are not toys. Do not use these machines unless supervised by your grandchildren.

CHAPTER 27:

Education: Long Summer Vacations, Plus the Chance to Make Someone as Miserable as Your Teachers Made You

A Bit of Historical Background

In the "Good Old Days," an idyllic period of our national life starting around the Civil War and extending up through the Jim Crow/lynching period, the Depression, and finally World War Two, young (white) Americans had the benefit of truly excellent teachers. This was because approximately half of the adult population (women) had no career options other than teaching. No matter how smart and ambitious you were, if you were a woman and wished to venture out beyond the home, you were pretty much going to be a teacher and accept whatever horrible pay was available for that job. This was known as the era of the idealistic or "dedicated" teacher.

Bad News

☹ Unfortunately, in the second half of the 20th century other opportunities opened up for women, offering a lot more money and prestige than teaching. Soon we could no longer count on excellent teachers willing to work for nothing. As a result there was a catastrophic decline in the quality of education.

GOOD NEWS

☺ But today, we have made education our number one national priority again! We're committing **massive resources** to this vital area, mainly in the form of **testing**. This means that while we still won't pay our teachers well, at least we're going to know just exactly how bad things have gotten, and we'll have the statistics to prove it.

WHAT YOU CAN DO

This is a "no-brainer!" *You* can become a teacher! You will have the gratitude of all good Americans if you choose this career! Especially if you don't complain too much about the salary, and all the time you'll be wasting preparing your students for the national tests we are making them take, to show what a commitment we've made towards education.

DISADVANTAGES

☹ You'll be overworked and underpaid.

☹ Most of your students will regard you with surly resentment.

☹ The school administration will regard you with fear and suspicion.

☹ You will be working either in crumbling, inner city neighborhoods where angry, poor kids have **dangerous weapons**, or in antiseptic, suburban neighborhoods where spoiled, rich kids have **dangerous lawyers**.

POSSIBLE ADVANTAGES

☺ Perhaps, against all odds, you could make the world a better place.

DEFINITE ADVANTAGES

☺ Summer vacation.

Having spent your entire life in school, you are uniquely positioned to understand what good teaching is all about.

You have certainly been subjected to poor teaching at one time or another: the crushing disappointment of sitting through **boring** classes taught by **uninspired** teachers, too inexperienced to know what they're doing, or so **beaten down** by life they were past all caring, not to mention teachers whose only joy was malicious, arbitrary judgment meted out in retaliation for the real or imagined injuries they have suffered in their lives, for which *you* were blamed and **punished.**

Thus, by becoming a teacher, you have the opportunity to take this unjust punishment which was visited upon you, and **pass it on** to the next generation! It's payback time!

No, wait! What we *meant* to say is that now you have the opportunity to *break* this vicious cycle of incompetence and become a truly great teacher. Just try to stay away from those dangerous, depressing places called "schools."

SUMMARY FOR STUDENTS

Fresh from twenty years' experience of seeing, from a student's perspective, just how mediocre education can be, how saturated it is with myths and omissions, you are in a perfect position to GET OUT NOW BEFORE IT'S TOO LATE!

SUMMARY FOR PARENTS

If everyone would just go back to the Good Old Days when kids didn't backsass their parents, and before this whole women's lib song and dance, we would have better schools and a stronger military.

CHAPTER 28:

A Career in Law Enforcement: Do You Have Any Idea How Fast You Were Reading?

Law Enforcement Aptitude Questionnaire

Have you always wanted to help and protect other people?	Yes	No
Do you have an ability to defuse potentially dangerous confrontations?	Yes	No
Do you enjoy hitting other people with clubs?	Yes	No

If you answered "yes" to any of the above questions, a career in law enforcement could be an excellent choice for you!

Pros

☺ You get to hang out with the coolest people society has to offer, since you're arresting them. This includes actors, rock stars, athletes, celebrities, CEOs—people who would never have hung out with you in college.

☺ You get to win every argument.

☺ You get to be extremely polite to people while you're giving them a very hard time.

Cons

☹ You have to enforce laws that seem arbitrary and unjust.

PROS

☺ That just makes it more fun.

CONS

☹ You have to tell people about their Constitutional rights.

PROS

☺ But not anymore.

CONS

☹ You have to show people a search warrant before you search their house.

PROS

☺ Nobody cares about that one anymore either.

MORE PROS

☺ Fast cars, motorcycles, high speed chases!

CONS

☹ The better criminals have faster cars than you do.

PROS

☺ You get to look hot in your powerful cop outfit.

CONS

☹ You're only supposed to beat on criminals.

MORE PROS

☺ You get to hang out with dogs who are, in some ways, arguably smarter than you.

☺ Little kids look up to you.

HOWEVER

☹ Little kids also look up to Bugs Bunny.

GETTING BACK TO THOSE PROS

☺ You get to confiscate massive quantities of drugs, and keep some if you like.

☺ You get to have arguments with some of the dumbest people in America.

☺ You could be on one of those "Real Cops" type TV shows.

ON THE OTHER HAND

☹ You might end up on one of those "Real Cops" type TV shows.

☹ The criminals all have automatic weapons and all you have is a .38, plus your commanders are always trying to get you to use non-lethal weapons like stun guns, beanbags, rubber bullets, etc.

BUT

☺ They don't really care if you use them. Actually, they'd prefer that you didn't.

BACK TO THE NEGATIVES

☹ You wind up in the middle of screaming family fights you joined the police force to escape.

☹ Unbelievable amount of detailed paperwork in which you have to describe exactly what happened when you apprehended a suspect.

BUT ON THE POSITIVE SIDE

☺ You can lie about it.

CONS

☹ You'll get criticized unfairly by snotty liberals for every little mistake you make.

☹ You have to break up parties.

☹ You're supposed to have "probable cause" to search somebody or stop a vehicle.

PROS

☺ "Probable cause" can probably be almost anything.

BAD NEWS

☹ Your role is limited to dealing with the symptoms rather than the root causes of crime in our society.

GOOD NEWS

☺ Who cares?

FUN THINGS YOU CAN DO TO SUSPECTS

1. Tell them their buddies are going to testify against them; see what happens.
2. You can be the "good cop" or the "bad cop" in the good cop/bad cop routine.
3. When you arrest someone, you can do a really bad job of protecting their head from hitting the roof of the patrol car.
4. Invent your own field sobriety tests. (Example: put your finger on your nose, stand on your head, and recite the "Pledge of Allegiance" backwards.)

SUMMARY FOR STUDENTS

Great career choice for you if you're someone with a heroic personality and a strong desire to protect, serve and totally dominate your fellow citizens.

SUMMARY FOR PARENTS

There may be reasons why you don't want your child to go into law enforcement, but imagine how much fun it could be to scold a cop!

CHAPTER 29:

CAREERS IN PSYCHOLOGY & COUNSELING: HANGING AROUND WITH PEOPLE EVEN MORE SCREWED UP THAN YOU

You may think that because you have **major psychological problems**, you are well suited for a career as a therapist. This is a myth. You are much better suited for a career as Attorney General of the United States.

But if you like hanging out with really screwed up people, this may be the career for you. The father of modern psychology, **Sigmund Freud**, spent so much time with really screwed up people that he was rumored to have used cocaine in his off hours to relieve the tension. Actually, this is also a myth. The truth is Freud was coked out for the majority of his working *and* his free hours. So you're beginning to think maybe this *is* the field for you after all. But you'll need years of training in order to transform your amateurish terminology and advice into fully professional diagnosis and treatment. If you'd prefer to skip the years of training, you can just memorize this simple list:

Everyday Terminology	Professional Diagnosis	Treatment
Crazy as a loon	Dissociative disorder	Psychotherapy
Not playing with a full deck	Psychopathic personality	Psychoanalysis
Nutty as a fruitcake	Bipolar disorder	Lithium
Not rowing with both oars in the water	Anxiety disorder	Prozac
Lights on, nobody home	Dementia	More tests
Voices in my head	Schizoid personality with paranoid delusions	Horse tranquilizers
Uniquely creative	Attention deficit disorder	Horse tranquilizers

Of course some patients are resistant to these modern approaches, and in certain cases the therapist may opt for more **traditional methods**, such as drilling holes in their heads to let the evil spirits out. You might want to try this at home.

"Yes," we hear you saying, "but do I have the patience and discipline to listen to crazy people complaining all day?" The answer is: yes, you do. In fact, you're probably already doing it, the only difference being you're not making any money off it. Consider the following:

Venue: Your Dorm Room (Time: 2:00 A.M.)

YOUR FRIEND
Blah, blah, blah, blah, blah.

YOU
Oh, that's terrible. That must be really hard for you.

YOUR FRIEND
Yadayadayadayada.

Venue: Your Office (Time: 10:00 A.M.)

YOUR PATIENT
Blah, blah, blah, blah, blah.

YOU
Oh, that's terrible. That must be really hard for you.

YOUR PATIENT
Yadayadayadayada.

YOU
Gee, that's harsh. Here, have a beer.

YOU
I can tell you're in a lot of pain. Here, have a heterocyclic antidepressant, and come back for another session in a week.

Total income from exchange: $0.00

Total income from exchange: $150.00

Now you are eager to become a professional therapist. But first, you'll want to fill out this questionnaire to determine if your preparation, natural abilities and personality type are a good match for a career in clinical psychology.

PSYCHOLOGY APTITUDE QUESTIONNAIRE

What have you studied so far in the field of Psychology?

How does that make you feel?

Really? That's interesting.

Yes, go on.

Please continue.

Had any dreams lately about being a psychologist?

That's *very* interesting. How did that make you feel?

Well, our time is up. Just leave the check at the door.

One of the earliest innovations in the field of psychology was the Rorschach test, in which the patient is shown a randomly generated ink blot, then asked to say what it reminds him of. The test reveals what is on the patient's mind, and can be a useful tool in the exploration of subconscious wishes, desires and fears. You may experiment with the Rorschach test on the following page. What comes immediately to mind when you see this?

RORSCHACH TEST

Be truthful: we can't help you if you're going to lie about this.

THE FREUDIAN SLIP

Sometimes psychologists are able to learn more about what is really on a patient's mind by listening for accidentally misstated phrases or incorrect usage of a word. This is known as a Freudian slip. The patient may not realize they have misspoken unless it is pointed out by a highly trained professional. Keep a close eye out—sometimes these "slips" donkey sex are very, very subtle. Moving on:

SUMMARY FOR STUDENTS

Any in-depth study of psychology reveals that your behavior is the result of a complex interplay between genetic and environmental factors, sometimes called nature and nurture, or more simply:

SUMMARY FOR PARENTS

It's all your fault.

CHAPTER 30:

A CAREER IN SHOW BUSINESS

Note to Film Majors: You Are More Skilled, Knowledgeable and Prepared for Your Career Than Any Previous Generation! (Alert: Nobody Cares!)

THE GOOD NEWS

☺ In the last twenty years there has been an explosion of interest on college and university campuses in the United States in the glamorous and exciting fields of film, television and music.

This means that if you have an interest in pursuing a show business career, you'll have taken numerous courses, deepening your **knowledge** of the history and inner workings of the Industry, while acquiring hands-on **experience** in writing, producing, directing, acting in and editing your own student films!

THE BAD NEWS

☹ As dramatically foreshadowed above...nobody cares.

MORE GOOD NEWS

☺ Despite the fact that it is notoriously hard to "break in" to show business, there are actually quite a lot of nurturing, caring, successful producers, writers, actors, directors, studio and network executives who are really **interested** in meeting and talking with you, and who would like to see your student film!

MORE BAD NEWS

☹ They're lying. (They couldn't care less about you, and they certainly don't want to see your student film.)

BUT WHY WOULD THEY LIE ABOUT SOMETHING LIKE THAT?

The answer to that question is another bit of

GOOD NEWS

☺ There are many, many successful producers, writers, actors, directors, studio and network executives who have a deep and **sincere** interest in film schools, and programs devoted to the Industry on campuses all over the country. The reason they are deeply and sincerely interested is, however, another bit of

BAD NEWS

☹ They are hoping to **find jobs** teaching film courses in these colleges and universities when they reach the Showbiz Mandatory Retirement Age of 28. Squirreled away within this piece of bad news, fortunately, is yet another piece of

GOOD NEWS

☺ As a recent graduate, you are very likely several years younger than the Mandatory Retirement Age of 28! So this is the **perfect time** to break down that door and get your exciting showbiz career started!

The very best thing you can do in this effort is to have a very close member of your immediate **family** (mother or father preferred, sister or brother acceptable) be a **powerful** person in the Entertainment Industry. For example, here's a quick exercise that could help a lot:

→ Take out your drivers license, and see if your last name is "Douglas." No? Too bad. "Baldwin?" "Bridges?" No? Well, it never hurts to be sure. How about "Spielberg?" Just checking.

If your last name is not Douglas or Baldwin or Bridges or Spielberg, run—do not walk—to the nearest telephone and contact your **parents** immediately, informing them of how **urgent** it is that they become powerful people in the Entertainment Industry.

WHAT IF MY PARENTS FAIL TO BECOME POWERFUL PEOPLE IN SHOW BUSINESS?

★ Negative thinking is not encouraged in this book.

★ However, if your parents let you down, there still is one more piece of

GOOD NEWS

☺ Your **best friend's** mother or father is a powerful person in show business!

BUT I DON'T HAVE A BEST FRIEND LIKE THAT

Get one!

Good luck.

NOTE FOR ACTORS

As you may have noticed, television, and now movies, are being taken over by "reality shows" which means, unfortunately, that there are **no** longer any **jobs** for actors. This new trend does, however, open up a new career opportunity for you as a real person in a reality show or movie.

VOCABULARY ALERT

A **real person** is someone who lives in a completely fabricated living environment, with an entirely fabricated social life, consisting of other real people who fabricate their emotional responses to each other in order to be briefly famous and possibly win money.

If you think you have the talent needed to portray yourself, if you could pretend to care about people you've just met, get upset about things that don't matter, and if you'd enjoy being publicly humiliated in front of millions of your peers, this could be just the thing for you.

EXCITING ALTERNATIVES TO MAINSTREAM ENTERTAINMENT

While there are no jobs in the crass, commercial wasteland of Hollywood, there are plenty of jobs in the expanding culture of **Independent Film Making!** In this field you can exercise maximum **creative control**, use real actors and writers, and express your personal **vision.**

Of course, you won't make a dime and nobody will ever see your film, and if they did, they probably wouldn't like it, or even stay until the end, which is especially insulting considering most Independent Films are like, 13 minutes, but in the long run, art is its own reward, right?

SUMMARY FOR STUDENTS

As a film major you now have the knowledge, skills, experience and talent to marry into a powerful showbiz family. What are you waiting for?

SUMMARY FOR PARENTS

You may be disappointed that your talented film major may have to start off her career at an "entry level" position, like, say, "parking attendant." Don't be. She's already doing better than the Philosophy Majors.

CHAPTER 31:

STARTING A BAND: WHY NOT JUST ROLL AROUND NAKED ON BROKEN GLASS?

In the wonderful world of art there is endless potential. You could be the creator of the soothing tunes we all turn to for comfort and inspiration, the soft sounds of the human voice reflecting our greatest insights and emotions, our joys and our sorrows.

Or you could be a musician.

VOCABULARY ALERT

A **musician** is a person culturally deemed to be outstandingly good-looking, who uses his/her good looks to sell albums.

The current buzzword in the music industry is **raw talent**. This can be good or bad news. If you are a beginning musician, or not a musician at all, you may have huge amounts of untapped "raw talent." On the other hand, if you are an experienced musician, or you foolishly studied music in college, you may have a little work ahead of you.

WAYS TO IMPROVE YOUR RAW TALENT AND GET RID OF SOME OF THAT EXCESS ACTUAL TALENT

1) Turn off the CD player and turn on the radio. The radio is a rich source of examples of bands with lots of raw talent.

2) Bash your head against a wall a bunch of times. As your total number of brain cells decreases, your raw talent inversely and proportionally increases.[10]

If you're new to the music world and need to catch up quickly with other bands who have more experience, try:

THINGS YOU CAN DO TO MAKE YOUR BAND SOUND BETTER

Play louder.
Smoke pot.
Get drunk.
Take hallucinogens.
Play a lot louder.

There! Now your music is starting to sound a lot better. But you still need to develop a unique and original style.

THINGS YOU CAN DO TO IMPROVE YOUR MUSICAL STYLE

Become anorexic.
Breast implants (get).
Dreads or other cool hairdo.

Abuse your vocal cords to the point that your voice sounds more like a car starting than anything that could possibly be produced by a human being.

COLLABORATION

Beyond the joy of making music is the deeper and ultimately more satisfying joy of collaborating with other members of your band. Over time you develop a sixth sense for the unique talents of each musician in the group so that the whole

---

[10]Warning: Not that hard! You need to apply the maximum force *without* causing permanent skull damage which could prevent you from performing, or getting out of bed, an essential part of being a good musician.

is more than just the sum of the parts. Eventually you can't even recall who contributed what in the creation of a song; you can't honestly say where you end and the others begin.

But enough joking around.

In reality, there can be only **one** creative genius in every band, and that genius is you.

The others can express themselves by playing your music, the way you want it played.

WAYS TO GET RID OF SOMEONE WHO ISN'T PLAYING YOUR MUSIC THE WAY YOU WANT IT PLAYED

You're on the brink of stardom, but your bass player is holding you back. You should:

1. Call a practice, don't tell him about it, then get really mad at him for not showing up.
2. Conduct a surprise drug test.

OTHER CAREERS IN MUSIC

A sensible musician at one point or another often considers compromising his original intention of being a rock star and going into a related field such as **music recording**. Of course, most musicians don't want to be small players in the big corporate scheme to destroy all decent music on the planet. So they consider creating an independent label, i.e. their own studio.

GOOD NEWS

☺ Decide your own hours.

☺ No boss.

☺ Studio in the convenience of your back yard.

☺ Work directly with fresh, new talent; help them make it big.

BAD NEWS

☹ Your clientele are possibly *the* brokest people on earth.

GOOD NEWS

☺ You don't really care about your clientele, because you secretly plan to use your studio to push your own music career.

BAD NEWS

☹ The people who loaned you the money to build your studio enjoy watching artists' dreams shatter in their greedy hands, and will bulldoze your studio the day you are late for a payment.

SUMMARY FOR STUDENTS

If, after reading this chapter, you still want to be a musician, it shows you have a passionate love of and commitment to your music, and you are certifiably insane.

SUMMARY FOR PARENTS

If we didn't provide adequate advice about careers in the area of your own musical interest, such as classical, jazz, world or any of the other styles of our rich, cultural tradition, please be assured it is only because our space is limited, and also, nobody cares, you are living in the past, and your music sucks.[11]

---

[11] We also neglected Rap. But we love Rap. Please do not come to our house with guns.

While you're waiting for your band to get signed or that Big Break into Show Biz, which we know is going to happen very soon, you will need to pay the rent. But you want to be able to drop your day job in the blink of an eye when that Big Break comes, which is why we're pulling another helpful chapter from the advanced, "Jobs You Can Actually Get" section.

CHAPTER 46:

TEMP WORK: NOT SO GREAT, BUT IT'S ONLY TEMPORARY!

Temp work is an excellent way to get started in the working world. It allows you to sample a **variety** of different kinds of jobs, exposing you to multiple work environments. It's short term employment, temp agencies value the skills you've learned in college, and if you don't want to work through an agency, you can simply situate yourself with the other college graduates standing on the **corner** outside the nearest lumber yard, and watch for pickup trucks driving by slowly.

It's also extremely good if you're the employer. It means you can hire someone to fill in for a worker who is sick or on vacation, or even to do work that you would prefer not to do. Say there's a specific project that seems especially arduous or boring, but you said you'd do it, and it has to get done. Or maybe you're so damn **lazy** you just don't feel like showing up to work for a couple of days. Wouldn't it be nice to have somebody come in and do your job for you? For example:

Hi!

I just got hired to write this chapter. I'm not a writer or anything, actually I'm a musician or an actor, and I don't really know what I'm supposed to do, but the Agency sent me over, so I guess I'll just work until they fire me, like I always do.

They usually train me, but there's nobody here. There's just a note that says, "Write a chapter for a book about Temp Work. You will be fired when you're done."

So here I am.

Maybe I guess I'll just talk about what I know. Um— a bad thing about temp work: no benefits. But I guess it's a good thing if you're the boss.

Most people probably think getting fired is bad. But to me it's the best part of the day. It means I get to go home.

Quitting is even better. I get to tell my boss to take his job and shove it two or three times in a good week. Who else can say that?

You like dramatic exits? Try these:

1. Develop a rapidly degenerating mental illness.

2. Lose control of your left arm.

3. Recite a speech from your favorite movie, like Network ("I'm mad as Hell, and I'm not going to take it any more!") or Jerry McGuire ("These fish have manners. In fact they're coming with me. I'm starting a new company, and the fish are coming with me.") That one's my personal favorite—I've used it three times already this month.

4. Sing the lyrics to your favorite Metallica album.

Well, I'm tired of this job. I think I'm going to pee on my boss' desk and leave.

CHAPTER 32:

PROFESSIONAL SPORTS: PROS AND CONS OF LEAVING COLLEGE BEFORE YOU'VE COMPLETED ALL FOUR YEARS OF REMEDIAL READING

If you happen to be attending college on an athletic scholarship, perhaps playing on one of the better college football or basketball teams and looking forward to a lucrative career in one of the professional leagues, chances are you are **not reading** this book.

More likely it is being read to you by a friend. This brings up an important consideration: if a professional sports team has already offered you a huge signing bonus even though you may not have completed your four years of study, should you **accept** the offer now, and leave the ivied walls **without a college degree?**

Of course, no one can make this decision for you, but here are a few things to consider:

A career in professional sports can be wonderfully exciting, personally fulfilling, tremendously rewarding financially (and in many other ways), but it can also be extremely short. You are always one **knee injury** away from permanent retirement. That is why you may not want to leave college without first learning how to read. Reading is an enormously important life skill for the non-athlete, which you may become at any time when some other athlete steps on your knee.

On the other hand—and this is the hard part of the decision-making process—if that other athlete happens to step on your knee before you've graduated from college, you forfeit your entire pro career, with all the attendant perks, **before** you've made your first **million dollars**. This would be truly tragic, even more tragic than a shortened pro career following an aborted college education. Besides, there are plenty of people in our society who can read, and after a season or two in professional sports, you should have enough money to pay them to read to you for the rest of your life. Also, you will have plenty of time on your hands for hobbies, like learning how to read, once your playing days have come to an end, or somebody steps on your knee, whichever happens first.

But maybe you are not among the lucky few who must struggle with the decision of whether or not to leave college to accept a lucrative pro offer before you've learned how to read. Perhaps you are more the classic, well-rounded "student athlete," someone who competes purely for the love of the game, but who recognizes that there are more important things in life than sports, especially since **no pro team will take you**. You may even fit the profile of the "Rhodes Scholar."

VOCABULARY ALERT

A **Rhodes Scholar** is an outstanding student athlete eligible for the prestigious Rhodes Scholarship to Oxford University in England, due to excellent performance both on the field and off. If this sounds like you, you should definitely stay in school until you learn how to read.

Whether or not you have a future as a professional athlete, you will eventually need to consider:

OTHER JOBS IN SPORTS
Coaching

You may be surprised to learn that you don't have to be knowledgeable about sports or even minimally athletic in order to be a great coach. However, you must have a unique combination of interpersonal skills: rage, violent hostility, obsessive-compulsive disorder bordering on sociopathic anger, uncontrolled aggression, inability to distinguish between sports and reality, inability to accept defeat, inability to accept victory, and a really loud **screaming** voice. However, if you coach youngsters, like in Little League or AYSO, your sensitive spirit may be wounded by the *really* scary people: parents. (For your own protection you will need to be armed at all times.)

SUMMARY FOR STUDENTS

It's not that you **suck** at basketball, it's just that your mind is too valuable to be wasted on athletics.

SUMMARY FOR PARENTS

Your child is too small to play professional sports because of *your* mediocre DNA.

CHAPTER 33:

DREAM JOBS: GETTING PAID FOR WHAT YOU DO ANYWAY

You may think you're not qualified for a fabulous Dream Job like movie, restaurant or music critic, but the fact is, you're *already* all of those things, you just never realized it before!

All you really need to do is adjust your natural instinct for criticism to the accepted jargon of the profession, and **alakazam**, you're a critic!

For example:

What You Say Coming Out of a Movie Theater

Man, that movie totally sucked!

Professional Movie Critic

After exploring the dark nuances of the human spirit in her previous work, DIRECTOR'S NAME HERE has opted for a more conventional excursion into the contemporary thriller with political overtones, a reach which turns out to be a disappointment on several levels.

What You Say at a Sporting Event

Make a goddamn free throw, ya bum, ya!! Boo! You suck!

Professional Color Commentator

Looks like he's reverting to that stiff follow-through which was plaguing him earlier in the season.

What You Say Coming Out of a Restaurant

Dude! I am totally stuffed!

Professional Restaurant Critic

Chef NAME OF CHEF HERE has finally emerged from the shadow of NAME OF ANOTHER CHEF HERE, for whom he worked as a *sous chef* at NAME OF RESTAURANT HERE. At his new venue, he has combined the robust herbs of his native NAME OF COUNTRY HERE with the delicate sauces of *nouveau cuisine* to create an exhilarating experience which lingers on the tongue.

What You Say Coming Out of a Rock Concert

That guitar player was like: danh, danh, dadanh danhda! and the drummer was all, bapa-dadubladudbablbltu, and the bass player was like bowm, du bowm, bowm, and that singer was just going Rwaaawhhh!!

Professional Music Critic

That band totally sucked.

So you see how well qualified you are, it's only a matter of getting hired. As for that, you're on your own. We can't do everything for you.

However, here's a hint for you if you're an aspiring movie critic:
1. Pick a horrible movie. The worst one you can find.
2. Write a great review. Use phrases like, "Two Thumbs Up!" "Biggest Hit of the Summer!" "A Must-See!" "If you see only one movie this year..." "Wow!"
3. Sit back and see yourself quoted in every newspaper ad in the country. You're on your way to a dream career.

SUMMARY FOR STUDENTS

Nobody likes a critic, but your dream job isn't about being liked, it's about being **feared**. Isn't that better than being liked?

SUMMARY FOR PARENTS

If you've ever complained about anything at a restaurant—the location of your table, how well cooked your food is, how promptly it's delivered, the suitability of the wine, anything at all—you might make a good restaurant critic, but probably you're just a jerk (see chapter on Waiting Tables).

CHAPTER 34:

CRIME: THE MOST LUCRATIVE PROFESSION FOR WHICH THERE ARE NO FORMAL REQUIREMENTS[12]

Talk about excitement! There is really no competition in the adventure/excitement area to the life of the professional criminal. And that's just the beginning!

THE GOOD NEWS

☺ There is no more intriguing figure in today's popular culture than the **lovable** hit man or hit woman. Due to advances in modern entertainment technology we now know that most violent criminals are witty, intelligent, thoughtful, caring, affable and sincere.

☺ No taxes! Well, technically, there are taxes, but they have to catch you first!

☺ You get to meet a lot of **interesting people**, whose fashion styles will be six months ahead of the curve.

☺ While many other sectors have struggled to keep pace with the cost of living, the price of a hit just keeps going up and up.

☺ If homicide isn't your thing, there's also extortion, loan sharking, illegal gambling, prostitution, drugs, embezzlement, the list goes on forever, and is limited only by your own imagi-

---

[12]You may feel unprepared for a life of crime, but if you've been benefiting from the many advantages of dorm life, chances are you've got enough stolen MP3s on your hard drive to open up a black market in Sri Lanka.

nation and resourcefulness! And a college education is a big plus in the area of **white collar crime**, by far the most rewarding and least dangerous form of illegal activity.

☺ When the novelty begins to wear thin, there are wonderful opportunities to make tons of money writing about your crimes in **books, movies and TV shows.**

☺ If exploiting your experience for its entertainment value violates your ethical standards, another secondary career available to you when your peak earning years are over is a career as a Government Informant. Among the perks of this second crime career is the **Witness Protection Program** run by the Justice Department, where you will be given a new identity and a new job in a new location, far away from where you are now. If you're lucky, you may even get a new family. (And who wouldn't like a new family now and then?)

However, it would be irresponsible to list the many advantages of this line of work without also acknowledging the fact that there are also disadvantages, so we urge you, particularly if you are attracted to a life of crime, to pay careful attention to:

The Bad News

☹ No pension.

Crime, Part Two—Politics: Extending Your Criminal Career When You're Too Old for Murder, Extortion, Armed Robbery and Kidnapping

The lack of a good pension is one of the reasons you will want to explore extending your criminal career into the related field of politics, where there are outstanding pensions available. But there's so much more!

The Good News

☺ (See Chapter 39: Internships)

☺ Whenever your freedom to pursue your criminal lifestyle is threatened by an all too rigid legalism (law), you can **change the law**! That, after all, is what you've been elected to do.

☺ If it seems like you're not making enough money, you can **raise your own salary**! This is typically done late at night at the end of a Congressional session and is not covered by the media!

☺ If it's still not enough money, you can generally rely on **lobbyists** to help you out in exchange for your help with some legislation they know a lot more about than you do anyway.

☺ As long as you remember to call them "fact-finding expeditions," your frequent vacations to the world's most luxurious resorts and exotic locations are **fully paid for** by the taxpayers! Also, you get to go there in comfortable corporate jets! However, once again, it would be irresponsible of us not to point out:

THE BAD NEWS

☹ You have to get elected. But with your solid background in crime, you should be able to **steal** an election with some help from your criminal associates on the Supreme Court.

SUMMARY FOR STUDENTS

Most recent graduates have only been of voting age for a short period of time. Thus, the fact that our government is run by thugs, crooks and swindlers is not entirely your fault.

SUMMARY FOR PARENTS

It is, on the other hand, *your* fault.

CHAPTER 35:

CAREERS IN RELIGION: BUY 10 MORE COPIES OF THIS BOOK AND YOUR SINS ARE FORGIVEN

In any group of people there are some with a higher moral vision who hear the **call** to serve God. These special individuals use their extraordinary compassion and leadership to raise the moral bar, reminding us by their example of the rewards of self-sacrifice, self-denial, discipline and commitment to spiritual values.

Others become religious leaders.

VOCABULARY ALERT

A **religious leader** is someone who can describe the rewards of virtue in sermons so crushingly boring they just about guarantee the everlasting permanence of sin.

There are many advantages to the religious life. Even though you must set yourself apart to some degree from others, you have an opportunity to be God's servant on earth, to inspire hope among the hopeless, to pursue Enlightenment, and on top of all of this, you don't have to pay **taxes**.

But you might be thinking: I've led a less than perfect life while at college. How could I qualify to be a religious leader? The fact is, many sinners have become saints after leading a life of moral dissipation, once they realized the error of their ways. One of the most famous is Saint Augustine, who was a notorious sinner in his youth. The key here is not what you may have done in the past, but the sincerity of your **repentance**.[13] All religions are pretty similar in this regard, but the Catholic Church has one of the most accessible programs for repentance, called Confession.

In this ritual, you confess your sins to a highly trained **religious professional** who is qualified not only to hear your darkest thoughts and deeds, but also to guide you on the path towards God's forgiveness. You step into a Confessional and have a conversation like this:

> YOU
>
> Forgive me, Father, for I have sinned.

> PRIEST
>
> How long has it been since your last confession?

> YOU
>
> A long time—I've been in college the last four years. I've had impure thoughts.

> PRIEST
>
> What were you wearing at the time?

> YOU
>
> I don't know—probably a shirt and a—

> PRIEST
>
> Was it a sexy shirt?

> YOU
>
> I don't think that has anything—

> PRIEST
>
> A sexy penitent like you should be wearing sexy shirts, you know.

---

[13]Hint: There's no reason to rush into the repentance thing before you've fully sampled all the possible sins you will later repent. Remember, you can live a whole lifetime of sinning, so long as you repent in the end.

YOU
I don't think this is the place for me to find forgiveness.

PRIEST
How about my quarters later tonight, say around 8:00?

Once your sins have been forgiven, you can begin the training which will eventually equip you to take a place in the hierarchy of one of the worlds' great faiths. Although this training can be rigorous, you will persevere, knowing that religious **faith** has been the inspiration for the world's greatest works of art, most sublime compositions of music, most beautiful poetry, and most horrible **wars**.

But which faith is the right one for you? The following chart will help you choose:

RELIGIOUS LEADER LIFESTYLE COMPARISON CHART

	Sex	Hours	Benefits	Afterlife
Priest	Officially no, but...	Long	Tons	Yes, includes meeting St. Peter, God, others, angels singing in clouds with golden harps, but ☹ Hell also possible
Rabbi	OK	Long	Generally yes	No
Minister	Yep	Longish	Decent	Yes, but watch out for ☹ Satan
Imam	Yessiree	Long	Some	Garden with flowing streams, luscious fruits, richly covered couches and beautiful maidens,[14] but ☹ Hell also possible
Cult Leader	Unlimited	Set Own Hours	No guarantees	Up to you

[14]World Book Encyclopedia, 1995

SUMMARY FOR STUDENTS

When applying for a position in organized religion, be sure to mention any visions and/or conversations you have had with God. Note: for this career ONLY!

SUMMARY FOR PARENTS

If you've made it to the end of this chapter without being **offended**, it's probably because we've neglected to mention your own particular, second rate, primitive, good-for-nothing, bogus religion. There. Are you offended now?

CHAPTER 36:

A CAREER IN EDITING: DO WE REALLY NEED THIS CHAPTER?

There are two kinds of editors: the **copy editor** and the **creative editor**. If you're a good speller who pays close attention to detail, you could be an excellent copy editor. Unfortunately, copy editors are no longer needed thanks to the widespread use of quicker and more effective **Spell Check Pogroms**, which perform the same function, but for a faction of the cost.

So this leaves us with the general, or creative editor. Fortunately, you are already well-qualified for this career, because you've been editing your own writing throughout your college career. And you've probably also been editing others' writing.[15]

The function of the editor is to help the author organize, shape and present her material in the most advantageous and efficient manner, while helping the author find her own "voice." This is done mostly by "tightening" the often all too wordy prose. For example, let's suppose

---

[15]Sometimes called "plagiarism."

See how easy that was? We just "tightened" three pages into two! And nothing was missed.

If you've been paying closer attention to this book than we really would like, you may have noticed that several chapters mentioned in the Table of Contents do not, in fact, exist in the "body" of the work. This is because of some really first rate editing. Our editor reduced these overlong chapters from the **watery soup** they once were, to a thick, **rich broth**, boiling them down to their **essence**. As it happens, this turned out to be the chapter **titles**.

HANDY EXERCISES FOR EDITORS

Repeat the following phrases:
"Do we really need this?"
"This could go."
"Let's get rid of this whole section here."
"Lose it, Sparky."

SUMMARY, OR ALL YOU REALLY NEED TO KNOW ABOUT EDITING

Due to space limitations, this summary has been cut.

Mid Term Exam

1. Why is the field of medicine not covered in this book?

A) The doctor is unavailable to answer this question. You will have to ask one of the other doctors.

B) Who are also not available to answer this question.

C) If you are in medical school, you are not reading this book. If you are reading this book, you will never go to medical school.

2. What better way could you have spent the $11.95 you spent on this book?

A) Two minutes of professional help from a licensed therapist.

B) *Real Life, Here I Come!* an actual book of real advice for the college grad written by former Tennessee Homecoming Queen Autumn McAlpin, which includes helpful tips like what to do if your car engine catches on fire. (Helpful tip: Pull over, get out of car.)[16]

C) Small bottle of Stolichnaya or large bottle of Popov.

3. What is the most disappointing aspect of this book so far?

A) Absence of any actual helpful advice.

B) Still haven't come across promised, useful information which is certain to be in the next section, if you just keep reading.

C) Kevin Bacon never called back.

---

[16]page 118

4. How do I know other people are not cheating on this test?

A) The Pentagon's Total Information Awareness Office is monitoring their every move. As a matter of fact, they are also watching *your* every move, including what you are doing right now.

B) They are also monitoring your thoughts.

C) And they would like you to get your mind out of the gutter.

5. Ecology and Environmental Studies have not been closely examined in this book so far because:

A) The Environmental Impact Report isn't ready yet.

B) The EIR is ready, but hasn't been redacted yet.

C) The EIR is ready, has been redacted for National Security reasons, but has not yet been completely shredded.

6. Cultural Studies, an academic major also not covered so far in this book, is best defined as:

A) The deconstruction of hegemonic representation.

B) Representing hegemony in a deconstructive way.

C) Hegemonizing identity while deconstructing representation.

D) The academic discipline of how to NEVER find a job.

PART II: ESSAY QUESTION

(You only need to answer **one** of the following **three** essay questions)

A) Explain, in your own words, why your continued existence on the planet is justified by your performance in college. Be specific, citing examples of why you are not an expensive waste of space.

B) Explain, in your own words, exactly why you didn't want to answer A). Be very, very specific.

C) Why didn't you want to answer A) or B)? Why do we need to tell you again to *be specific*?

Send your test in to Santa Monica Press, P.O. Box 1076, Santa Monica, CA 90406, where it will be read and evaluated by the same, highly intelligent, trained chimpanzees who have been grading your midterms for the last four years.

(Remember, this test is for your benefit only. If, in spite of this, your first instinct is still to **cheat** or **lie** on any of these questions, you may have a bright future in Corporate Accounting, or possibly as a Security Analyst for a powerful Wall Street brokerage.)

SECTION FOUR

CHOOSING A REAL JOB ON THE BASIS OF WHAT YOU CAN ACTUALLY GET

CHAPTER 37:

Not Peaking Too Soon

OK. So you're not going to be a lawyer. It's probably for the better. Everything happens for a reason. Let's table our discussion of "careers" in favor of a more practical look at a "job."

But first let's consider some of the less well-known advantages of the "job" as opposed to the "career." Perhaps the most overlooked of these hidden benefits is that with a job you enjoy a remarkably reduced risk of peaking too soon in life.

We're all too familiar with the child star who, after a stunning success or two as a youth, disappears from sight, only to discover that she is officially a has-been before she's 30. She struggles through a few game shows and infomercials before a brief appearance on *Celebrity Boxing,* and then it's over. The best she can expect is having people come up to her and ask, "Didn't you used to be somebody?"

Let's hear from a few of these unfortunates.[17]

Can you match the following quotes with these celebrities who peaked too soon?

Former Celebrity	Quote
Mark Hammil	"I wish I had taken more time between *Son In Law* and *Bio-Dome.* Then maybe I could have understood more about myself."
Guy from 80's Hair Band	"I still don't get it. I was great in those movies, but I can't even get typecast these days."
Pauly Shore	"I object to being referred to as a generic representative of this category. I have a name and it's Gunner. Gunner Nelson, and my band, "Nelson," is not a has-been group, we're just not mainstream anymore. So #*!& off."

[17]For legal reasons, these quotes are presented in the form of a fun, interactive game!

The fact is, life is like a race, and while you may be more concerned right now with stumbling out of the starting gate, you really ought to be more concerned with **pacing** yourself, so that you have something left for the **stretch** run. When you're 30, or 40, you will still be looking brightly ahead, instead of regretfully behind you.

A similar dynamic is in play in the area of love and romance, not to mention sex, which is another topic entirely. This is not to suggest that you won't meet Mr. or Ms. Right tomorrow night. After all, unpredictability is one of the great things about the game of love. If you do meet him (or her) you should definitely grab him and, if necessary, handcuff him to a large piece of furniture in your apartment. However, the statistics on early marriage are not encouraging. This is due to **higher expectations** for love in your early twenties, as opposed to your early thirties.

Expectations at 20	Expectations at 30
Beautiful/handsome, charming, witty, smart, fun to be with, loves children, warm, caring, confident, dedicated, generous, capable, loving, strong, deep.	Better than the last guy.
Movie star good looks.	Has most of original teeth.
Somebody your parents will love.	Somebody you can bludgeon your parents into accepting.[18]

Not peaking too soon in life achievement is, conveniently, another way to increase your odds of not marrying too soon. To illustrate, here's a short **Pop Quiz**:

Which parts of this Engagement Announcement in the Society Page of the *New York Times* do **not** fit in with the rest, suggesting it is not, in fact, a genuine announcement?

Doctor and Mrs. Lionel Fitzgerald of Newport, Rhode Island, announce the engagement of their daughter,

---

[18]Suggested strategy: "You want grandchildren? Then shut up."

Penelope, to Christopher Hoskins Vanderbilt the third, son of Christopher Hoskins Vanderbilt Jr. and Elizabeth Montgomery Vanderbilt, of Falls Church, Virginia. The groom is a graduate of Yale Law school, and is currently employed as a busboy at the Captain's Wharf Bar and Grill in Newport. He will be joining the salad bar team in the fall. The bride is a graduate of Vassar College and is working as a telemarketer for Fabulous Vacations, Inc.

If you selected "busboy" and "telemarketer," you clearly understand how a job choice can affect the odds of a too-early marriage.

SUMMARY FOR PARENTS

If your graduate is unemployed or has taken a job which does not, in your opinion, measure up to your expectations, just be happy that at least she didn't rush into an unwise, early marriage.

SUMMARY FOR STUDENTS

On the other had, getting married early is a great way to prove something (to your parents, your friends, your enemies). Marrying for **love** is **overrated**. But marrying for **spite** is a lasting **satisfaction**.

CHAPTER 39:

Internships: Why Settle for Underpaid When You Can Be Not Paid at All?

A bit of history:

Back in the Good Old Days, when this country was governed by wise leaders who presided over a rich and good land of yeoman farmers, there was a word for the Internship Program. The word was **slavery**.

This system flourished for well over a century and played an important role in the development of our nation. But eventually, a bunch of troublemakers and outside agitators raised such a fuss about it that it was abolished, after a lengthy, and at times messy debate.[19]

So the first Great Internship Program was scrapped, and for many years people were paid for working. But then, due to the wonderful resourcefulness of the free enterprise system, which was mostly unfettered by burdensome **regulations** and other governmental interference, alternate methods were invented to move the engine of our economy along at maximum efficiency, like **child labor** and **sweatshops**. But then, you guessed it, those same agitators who spoiled the slavery thing started bellyaching again, and eventually passed another bunch of laws which prohibited these innovations, and then went even further

---

[19]Back then, people were allowed to question the wisdom of their leaders in a way which today would be considered unpatriotic, or even treasonous, but it was a time when news was spread mostly by rumor instead of by the Fox News Channel.

by passing the onerous **Minimum Wage Law.** It's a wonder that anything at all got done in this country after that.

But the ability to adapt to changing conditions is what continues to make this country great, and so today the innovators have come up with **Internships.**

Internships are popular mainly in the fields of Show Business, Journalism and Politics, but they are rapidly expanding into Law, High Finance and other desirable occupations. It's a great way for virtually anyone to get started on an upwardly mobile career path. Here is how it works:

1. A **mentor** puts out the word that an opportunity in a glamorous and powerful field is available to any bright, young college graduate with good connections, independent wealth and no other responsibilities.

2. The Intern gradually moves "up the ladder" from entry-level tasks like making **coffee** and answering phones, to more responsible work like getting sandwiches, copying, and even **shredding** important documents. The hours are long, the Intern is "on call" 24/7, superiors may sometimes be abusive, but in return for all the hard work and patient suffering, the Intern gets: **nothing.**

3. Just kidding. Actually, the Intern really does get something: **opportunity** and **connections**. If the college graduate shows an unusual amount of resourcefulness and ambition, it is often recognized and can easily become the first step on the Ladder to Success. An example is Monica Lewinsky, who went on to host an intelligent dating show in which a desirable bachelorette had to choose from a panel of bachelors whose identities were concealed behind **masks,** a direct result of her Internship in politics.

But even if you don't rise to the level of Monica Lewinsky, you still have a wonderful experience to beef up your resumé. You can describe it with powerful phrases like:

"I allowed myself to be ruthlessly exploited for six months for no pay by (NAME OF BIG SHOT). I made coffee and got sandwiches while aiding in the shredding of documents and covering up of affairs. I was yelled at and devalued as a human being by **very important people!**"

So what do the employers get out of all this? Actually, the term "employer" is incorrect. Since the "employee" is not paid, the relationship does not fall under the Minimum Wage Law, which is the genius of the arrangement. The correct term is "overseer." So what the overseer gets out of it is **free labor**.

If you have ever rushed for a fraternity or sorority and gone through the initiation process, you will have some prior experience in being exploited. There are similarities, but also differences:

	Fraternity/Sorority Initiation	Internship
Humiliation	☹ Yes	☹ Yes
Forced to drink dangerous quantities of alcohol	☹ Yes	☺ No
Subject to sexual abuse	☺ No	☹ Yes
Uncompensated labor	☹ Yes	☹ Yes
Eating live goldfish	☹ Yes	☺ Probably not
Eventual assimilation into elite group	☺ Yes	☹ No
Quality friendships which will last a lifetime	☹ No	☹ No
Chance to be on MTV	☺ Yes	☹ No

SUMMARY FOR STUDENTS

You may at one point or another, while managing your CEO's prescription drug addiction, ask yourself, "Am I really acquiring the knowledge and skills necessary to make it in (whatever field you're interning in)?" Hey, they're **not paying** you to ask questions.

SUMMARY FOR PARENTS

Everybody should have an intern. If you have any kind of business at all, definitely get one. There are so many college grads running around desperately seeking work, you can probably get one even if you don't have a business, or even if you're retired! Just tell 'em how great it'll look on their resumé.

CHAPTER 40:

DOING NOTHING

In our society, alas, doing nothing is not an acceptable ambition.

Historically, it has not always been this way. In 1847, a movement began in Philadelphia to make doing nothing acceptable. The leaders planned to **reinvent** society from the ground up, building an **infrastructure** more tolerant of those who don't do anything. Unfortunately, they never got around to doing any of this.

It's a shame these early efforts never got off the ground because doing nothing can be very productive and a great benefit for society. For example, think of how much better off we'd be if instead of doing what they did, **Adolf Hitler**, **Joseph Stalin**, and **Dennis Miller** had done nothing. Even in your own life you can probably think of instances when doing nothing, instead of what you actually did do, would have been a better choice.

★ In fact, people who actually **do** things spend most of their time **undoing** things that other people who do things have done. ★

Sadly, this dreary cycle is perpetuated when the people who do things discover that the things they have done have been undone by other people who do things, causing the original doers of the things to redo what was undone by the other doers. This, in turn, causes the undoers to reundo what the doers redid, and on and on and on.[20]

---

[20]A good example of this depressing phenomenon can be observed by reading *The Congressional Record* on any day of any year.

It doesn't take a rocket scientist to realize that if the people who do things would instead do nothing, then the other people who would have undone what the doers did would not feel obliged to undo anything, and could therefore also do nothing.

The bottom line: if you don't have anything good to do, don't do anything at all. And let's face it, you're not exactly **Martin Luther King, Jr.** So next time you're about to do something, ask yourself the question: Is what I'm about to do really any better than doing nothing?

Unfortunately, today, people who do nothing or aspire to do nothing are still stigmatized by society. They must do nothing "in the closet," fearful of "coming out" to declare themselves openly as who they really are. If you happen to be one of these people, you will need a "cover" for your real lifestyle.

For example:

TRAVEL

Traveling is a great hobby for the satisfied unemployed. You can literally *do* nothing, but *be* in another country, and people will respect that. Observe:

"What have you done since college?"

Unacceptable Response:
"I spent the last six months **doing nothing**."

Take out, "doing nothing" and add, "in Rome."
"I spent the last six months **in Rome**."

Sounds a lot better, eh? Not only is this now an acceptable response, it is also reusable:
"I'm spending the next six months **in South Africa**."

You just bought yourself another six months!

If traveling seems to be a bit more than you can comfortably fit in to your schedule of doing nothing, there is also:

WRITING

"What have you been doing since college?"

Acceptable Response:
"I'm in the **process** of writing a book."

Wow. Impressive.

But watch out for tricky questions, like:
"What is the book about?"

Try:
"That's a really good question. I'm in the process of **discovering** what the book is about myself. Just when I think I know, I discover a new level."

Sounds pretty deep. That should satisfy them. You are free to do nothing for a few more years.

The great thing about writing a novel is that the best novels often take decades to write. If, after four years, your answer to the what-are-you-doing question is still, "I'm writing a poem," chances are this will not go over well. But with a novel, you can be "writing" it for so many years that people forget exactly how long it's been, and 13 years seems more or less the same as six.[21]

The great thing about any kind of writing is "research." "I'm researching my book," is an acceptable answer to such questions as, "Why are you hiding from your family, friends and creditors under an assumed name in another country?" or "Why are you in prison?" Also, you can deduct any expenses you have incurred

---

[21]The same is true for a Ph.D. thesis. You can be working on your dissertation for literally your entire life and nobody will ever notice. After a while they will just stop asking when you think you'll finish.

from your taxes under the category of "research," since all aspects of life are really research for your book, are they not?

SUMMARY FOR STUDENTS

The real problem with doing nothing is it's very difficult to do. If you manage to actually do nothing, you may have already done too much.

SUMMARY FOR PARENTS

We're only kidding about your graduate aspiring to do **nothing** with that expensive college education. *Of course* they will do something with it, probably many things, sooner or later. Eventually.

Relax.

Take a few deep, cleansing breaths. **Visualize** your graduate doing something.

CHAPTER 41:

WAITING TABLES: IT'S NOT ROCKET SCIENCE, BUT THE TIPS ARE BETTER

There are basically two kinds of restaurants: the fancy, upscale places which offer foreign cuisine, and the friendly, family joints which offer basic American food.

Disadvantages of the Upscale Restaurant

The maitre'd is a jerk, the chef is a jerk, the other wait staff are all jerks, everybody speaks with a phony accent, most of the customers would look a lot better with that bottle of Chateauneuf du Pap '98 poured on their heads and a fondue fork driven through their hands.

Advantages of the Upscale Restaurant

Food's great, tips are terrific.

Disadvantages of Family Restaurant

Screaming kids, spilled drinks, no class, mediocre tips, lousy food.

Advantages of the Family Restaurant

Life changing experience if you're considering starting a family.

No matter which kind of establishment you end up in, your success will depend upon your ability to master the basic **vocabulary** of the waiter.

What You Feel Like Saying	What You Do Say
You want to know what salad dressings we have when I've *just* recited the whole list twice already for your bratty kids, and it's printed in big type on the menu right in front of your illiterate eyes, you know damn well what they are, since it's the same list as every other restaurant in town, and you always order the same thing anyway?!	We have French, thousand island, oil and vinegar, ranch, blue cheese, and Roquefort.
Your credit card has been declined, you big phony bastard, and I don't give a damn what your clients think about it.	I'm terribly sorry, but we're having some difficulty with our credit card machine. Do you happen to have another card?
There are people waiting for your table who are hungry and will give me tips, while you've been lounging over your coffee for the past half an hour. How'd you like to get your greedy, selfish, fat asses the hell out of here?	Is there anything at all I can get you? More coffee, another dessert, an after dinner liqueur, perhaps even more water?
Now that I've poured you a sip of this ridiculously overpriced bottle of swill you ordered, watching you pretend to evaluate its quality (as though you could tell the difference between a truly good wine and a bottle of spoiled vinegar) would be farcical if it wasn't so annoying.	Very good, sir. An excellent choice.
I'm going to spit in your food.	May I suggest the spinach soufflé?
You want me to take this steak back to the kitchen because it's undercooked? Do you realize I was the understudy for Hamlet in the Woodbridge Barn Theater summer stock production in 1998? Did you you know I was the Second Policeman in "You Can't Take It with You" in the Equity Waiver Theater Festival? And you want me to take this steak back to the kitchen?!	O! I die, Horatio; The potent poison quite o'er-crows my spirit: I cannot live to hear the news from England, But I do prophesy the election lights On Fontinbras: he has my dying voice; So tell him, with the occurents, more or less, Which have solicited— The rest is silence. [*dies*]

SUMMARY FOR STUDENTS

I'm sorry, we're out of chapter summaries for students tonight. May I suggest the chapter summary for parents?

SUMMARY FOR PARENTS

This chapter is underdone! We *specifically* ordered well-done, and you bring us this sorry excuse for a chapter. We can't read this. Take it back.

After waiting tables, graduate school is beginning to look a little better to you, isn't it? Maybe it's time to go back to Section One, "Plundering the Resources at Your College," for a chapter that you are now mature enough appreciate.

CHAPTER 8:

STAYING IN SCHOOL FOR ADVANCED STUDIES: GRAD SCHOOL, OR JUST REFUSING TO LEAVE YOUR DORM

Say you're a history major and your senior thesis was a comparison between Machiavelli's *The Prince* and Sun Tzu's *The Art of War*. This makes you an expert on manipulation, sabotage, lying, back-stabbing and betrayal, and more importantly, is excellent preparation for grad school.

Your expertise equips you to evaluate where the power is really located in your department, whether it's with the current Chairman and his allies, or one of the competing cabals vying for power.

Things move slowly in academe—chances are your Chairman is protected by generations of complex rules and procedures, **tenure** being only one of them, designed to protect and extend the power of the entrenched. It may be best for you to make a temporary **alliance** with the Chairman now, while going behind his back to suggest to the various pretenders to the Chair that you're really on their side, so when the ax falls at last, you can quickly switch allegiance to the new, stronger candidate. Then you may begin your campaign to undermine the new Chairman. Soon, you will have many friends and allies. Don't trust any of them.

But how to evaluate the strength of the Chairman? The following comparison chart should help:

Strong Chairman	Weak Chairman
Lots of published books, including textbook currently in use at the college.	Lots of published books, but textbook was replaced by competing textbook last time Chairman was on sabbatical or in the hospital.
Faculty-Administration Committee is currently reviewing the whole idea of tenure, but guess who is Chairman of the Committee?	Faculty-Administration Committee currently reviewing tenure, and he's not on it.
In charge of many Professional Organizations, on Peer Review Committees for publications, often quoted in the newspapers as an authority, stays as far away from undergraduates as humanly possible.	Voted most loved professor by undergraduates six years in a row.
Strong, feared, ruthless, wins battles by intimidation alone.	Wait a minute, that's not your department Chairman, that's Machiavelli. Time to get over your senior thesis.

GRADUATE SCHOOL LIFE

Other than the drinking and the drugs, you'll be surprised by how little graduate school life resembles undergraduate life. Instead of floating around campus trying to remember what courses you're supposed to be taking, you're going to have to teach, grade and do research for a Senior Faculty member who will then take all the credit for it. But you won't complain, because this Senior Faculty member is also Chairman of your Thesis Committee, and thus controls your entire destiny. This means you will gradually develop a seething resentment of this mentor, and if you happen to be in the Mathematics Department, you will have strong **homicidal urges** you will need to suppress with massive doses of **antidepressant medications**, which you should have at hand at all times.

If this seems like a lot of work for not much in the way of reward, (did we mention the pay for graduate assistants is lousy?) it is. But if you work hard, and find a master's and eventually a Ph.D. thesis topic that is so unutterably boring that nobody has ever thought of it before, you will eventually, after years of agonizing tedium and unrecognized labor, emerge from the university with a Doctor of Philosophy degree in something or other, which officially qualifies you to be called "Dr." and work in a fast food franchise.

ADVANCED STUDIES II: REFUSING TO LEAVE YOUR DORM

A much simpler approach to advanced studies is refusing to leave your dorm. Also, it doesn't require the industrial quantities of antidepressant medication so vital to making it through grad school. Consider it your own, personal Senior Gift to the college. But how to arrange it?

Living in the **laundry room** has its advantages. For one thing, you're so close to the washing machines, you might finally get around to cleaning your clothes, which you've been putting off for four years.

Also, you could use the washing machine for personal hygiene. (Wash in warm or cold water, set for Delicate Fabrics, Damp Dry → Avoid bleach!)

There are also the lounges. It's not unusual to see a student sleeping on a couch. That student could be you. Take a textbook, any textbook, spread it open on your chest, and go to sleep. Nobody will question you.

If you have trouble sleeping surrounded by the activity in the laundry room or the lounges, a good solution which involves no prescription drugs is attending Organic Chemistry lectures. After a good couple of hours, you should awaken refreshed and ready to take advantage of the cultural opportunities of campus life, which now no longer require a fake ID!

SUMMARY FOR STUDENTS

If the sometimes brutal competition and heartless pursuit of material reward offends your gentle, intellectual spirit, you should definitely avoid grad school in favor of the more idealistic path of selling used cars.

SUMMARY FOR PARENTS

While you should encourage the kid to follow her dreams, you should know that by the time she finishes her Ph.D., all of your friends will be dead, and there won't be anyone left to impress.

CHAPTER 42:

Winning the Lottery: Somebody Has to Win, Why Not You?

Have you ever been faced with the title of your term paper on the top of the page and right after that a totally **blank page** at 3:00 A.M. the morning the paper is due? Then you'll understand and appreciate just how much your college training has prepared you for the challenges you will face in the Real World.

You had to write, say, 5,000 words on the subject for your paper, and you had maybe 50. You may be surprised to discover that this corresponds with **actual situations** you could face in the Real World, like, say, having to write a chapter on Winning the Lottery for a book.

So what did you do?

First, you asked some important questions. For example: what, exactly, is meant by 5,000 words? How many pages is that? Do the spaces count? Do the spaces between paragraphs count? There are, ultimately, as many answers to these questions as there are professors in the world, so you had to conclude that basically, the definitive answer was **unknowable**.

But however many pages you estimated 5,000 words would be, it was surely more than the number you'd end up with by writing your 50 words. (Similarly, however many pages might be considered an acceptable chapter in a book, it would surely be more than one-half of a page, and probably more than one page.) And you didn't really have that much to say, or so it appeared at 3:00 A.M. Nevertheless, necessity being the mother of invention, you realized there were ways to **pad** and **stretch** those modest 50 words you could easily write on the subject, so that with a bit of luck, the length goal could be met.

What were those ways?

One way was to ask a lot of provocative **questions**, each of which would get **its very own line** on the paper. But more than that, there was the principle of statement and restatement, sometimes erroneously called the "dialectic,"[22] sometimes not. This principle states that if a thing can be said once, it can be said again. Put another way, one of the most effective essay techniques is the technique of repeated repetition. Put a third way, and this is one of the most commonly used guidelines in business presentations in the real world, "Tell them what you're going to say, say it, then tell them what you've said."

But what if you did all those things, and your paper *still* wasn't long enough?

Another option available was adding footnotes.[23]

At this point, you no doubt considered desperate measures, like screwing around with the margins, possibly even the font size or type. This would have two effects, a **desired** effect and an **undesired** effect. The desired effect would be that you would get to the end of the page a lot faster with the altered margins, font size and type. The undesired effect would be

[22]An electric dialing system developed for 19th century hand-held PDAs by G.W.F. Hegel.

[23]Although footnotes are generally in smaller fonts than the standard, they can still take up space at the bottom of the page.[24]

[24]It is also possible to add footnotes at the end of the paper, but this takes up less room.[25]

[25]"Good God! You didn't actually get a magnifying glass to read this, did you? Well, if you went to all that trouble, you deserve something in return. The winning lottery numbers are: 20-45-63-27. But you really need to get a life!"

that it would be really, really obvious to your professor, or to the graduate student who was reading the paper.

So you rejected that idea on moral grounds. However, you realized that if instead of screwing around with the margins or the font size, which was ethically wrong, you shaved a line or two from the top and bottom of each page, it would be a lot less obvious. It might not extend the page count as dramatically, but it would help, and you probably wouldn't get caught, which has a much higher level of integrity connected to it. Also, while your reader might not know why, your paper zipped along a bit faster than those of your peers, giving the added benefit of seeming to be written with greater energy and enthusiasm.

So, by using the principles of repetition, frequent provocative questions with their own paragraph breaks, repetition, shaving a few lines off the top and bottom margins, and repetition, you were able to finish that pesky term paper in time to meet the deadline, even if there wasn't a whole lot of time to spare.

SUMMARY FOR STUDENTS

Sorry, but there's no time for a Chapter Summary. This chapter had to be handed in a half an hour ago. Also, please don't contribute to the self-propagating, capitalist, false-hope-creating, dream-shattering death machine that is the U.S. lottery system. You won't win.

SUMMARY FOR PARENTS

You have two more kids to send to college: try your age divided by two, times six. And always pick 27.

(Chapter 43—Messenger Service: At Least You're Not in Some Office—was never delivered to the publisher because the messenger got lost.)

CHAPTER 44:

BEGGING: BEING YOUR OWN BOSS WHILE WORKING OUTDOORS— IT COULD BE WORSE

First, let's get rid of the stigma. There's nothing wrong with begging. It's one of the oldest professions. Plus, it's probably something you've been doing your entire life.[26] It's honest and straightforward, and perfectly legal in most places. You may think all beggars are on the lowest rung of society, but **studies** have shown that, next to waiting tables, begging is the most common form of employment immediately after college, and *the* most common employment after graduate school. So get over your stereotypes, get out there and hit the streets. The world awaits you, and the weather is fine.

POSITIVE ASPECTS OF A CAREER IN BEGGING
- ☺ Set your own hours.
- ☺ No formal training.
- ☺ No resumé.

---

[26]If you're a guy, it's probably how you lost your virginity.

☺ No references.

☺ Communication skills learned in college give you an immediate advantage over the competition.

☺ No office politics.

☺ Meet interesting people.

☺ Can't be fired.

☺ No dress code.

☺ Clear conscience.

☺ Great preparation for many other fields, such as:

BEGGING, PART TWO: WORKING FOR A NONPROFIT

If you're considering employment with a nonprofit, chances are you're an idealistic person with a strong desire to help humanity and piss off your parents. No, *of course* your parents will be proud of you. They understand you are sacrificing the possibility of a higher-paying job because you couldn't find one.

The fact is, most of the jobs you will get after graduating will feel like nonprofit. Many of these jobs will be nonprofit because your boss has taken all the profits, leaving none for anybody else. Hence the name "nonprofit" which actually should be, "not profitable for you."

Even if you haven't prepared for working at a nonprofit by begging on a street corner, you've probably already had lots of experience begging your family and friends for money, experience which can be put to use **fundraising** and writing **grant proposals**, the main activity of non-profits.

Of course, it helps if your nonprofit is proposing grants for "hot" areas. If you keep your finger to the wind, you'll be able to identify areas in which grant proposals are most likely to be funded at any given time, regardless of how well they're written.

Hot Areas	Not Hot Areas
☺ Faith-based cures for homo-sexuality and other disorders	☹ Bilingual education

☺ Environmental restoration, ecological preservation and habitat repair for golf courses

☺ Counseling, therapy and reintegration for majority groups displaced by affirmative action

☹ Community-based park development

☹ Social services for homeless

SUMMARY FOR STUDENTS

Begging and working for a nonprofit have a kind of symbiotic relationship. What beggars can't get on the street, they can sometimes get from nonprofit corporations which provide services to the needy. Conversely, if you work for a nonprofit, you will probably want to supplement your income by begging on the street.

SUMMARY FOR PARENTS

Begging isn't the only way to pay for college. There's also beachcombing with a metal detector.

CHAPTER 45:

TELEMARKETING: COULD NOT BE WORSE

In spite of what you may have heard, Telemarketing is actually one of the **best** jobs you can get right after college. Burnout and high turnover create a lot of openings, and if you like to talk on the telephone and are a good communicator, this could actually be a terrific opportunity.

"But I don't have time to waste looking into this dead-end career," you say.

The fact is: this won't take a lot of time. If you just give us a *moment* of your time, we'll explain how your earnings can actually multiply **tenfold** with telemarketing.

"Thanks, but I'm really more interested in psychology or business," you respond.

What *kind* of business are you interested in, 'cause you know, *every* business needs to advertise and there's no better way than to call people during dinner.

"Actually," you reply, "I *am* eating dinner right now—"

Yes, and we knew this would be a good time to catch you, and it's only going to take a *couple* of seconds to ask just a *few* questions which could dramatically improve your life.

"OK. Quickly."

How are you doing tonight?

"I'm fine, but I really—"

What's the one thing you are most dissatisfied about in your life?

"I *really* don't have time to read this right now," you say.

But we're almost finished! Just a *couple* more questions! You're doing great.

"I have to go now," you say.

Just one more question: If you could triple your income in the next ten seconds, would you do it?

"I suppose, but—"

That's great! Of course you would. And Telemarketing is a great way to do just that.

"I'm going to turn the page now—"

No! Don't turn the page! If we can tell you just **one** more thing about Telemarketing, we'll get credit for this chapter! Are you still there? Hello??

CHAPTER 47:

THE CLASSIFIEDS: NOW YOU'RE DESPERATE

Most people won't pick up the Classified Ads to look for a job until they're completely desperate, having exhausted all other avenues. However, one of the best kept **secrets** of the job market is that the Classifieds are actually a **great** way to find a great job.

For example, **Brad Pitt** got his first big break by responding to this ad:

> *Wanted: Male actor for lead role in major Hollywood motion picture. No experience required. High School diploma or G.E.D. preferred. Ask for Joe.*

Here's another ad that appeared in the Classifieds that was **overlooked** by most job-seekers in the market at the time who were "too smart" to waste their time looking in their newspapers.

> *State of Texas seeks Chief Executive. C average student, multiple business failures preferred, alcohol problem, AWOL OK, no drug test, no other qualifications required.*

You guessed it: our president, **George W. Bush**, got his first job in politics by responding to this ad. This was clearly a perfect match. But it requires patience and perseverance to find that ad which so clearly says "you." You may think you've found the perfect job:

Min wage, no bens, pick up trash in park. 8-10 yr exp,
Class A24 lic

But note special license and required experience you don't have! Another hidden pitfall to watch out for is the job which seems too easy to get: you may open the Classifieds and see an ad for a well paying job in the field of Armed Security. But before you accept this or any offer, it would be prudent to inquire, "What happened to the last guy?"

Good Answer
Promoted.

Bad Answer
Dead.

This information may be hard to extract, but don't let your potential employer off the hook with a vague answer. Ask where your predecessor is now.

Acceptable Response
He's right down the hall in his new, bigger office and he'd love to talk to you about your new job.

Unacceptable Response
Um, he's not around anymore. He went on to other things, someplace else. We're not supposed to talk about what happened.

Finally, be aware that the Classifieds are an excellent place to find cutting edge, **interdisciplinary** careers. If you've ever taken an interdisciplinary course in college, you know how the combination of two seemingly independent disciplines can form something totally new when brought together. For example, you could combine your passion for science with your interest in writing with a job as a **Science Writer**. Or unite your interest in sports with your premed training with a job in **Sports Medicine**. Or integrate your love of acting with your passion for talking on the telephone by answering one of the many classified ads for **Telephone Actress**.

If for some inexplicable reason you're not **fully satisfied** with your fabulous job as a Telephone Actress, you can upgrade your job search by taking advantage of the very latest technology described in our next chapter!

SUMMARY FOR STUDENTS

We don't actually know for a fact that George W. Bush got his first big job by reading the Classifieds. For that matter, we don't actually know that he can read.

SUMMARY FOR PARENTS

This is not meant as a knock on our President. He is a lovable character and a strong leader even if he probably can't read.

CHAPTER 48:

ONLINE JOB SEARCHING: YOU CAN BE HUMILIATED IN THE COMFORT OF YOUR OWN HOME

The big advantage of online job searching is that you can put out your resumé, knowing that it will be working for you 24 hours a day, seven days a week, even when you're **asleep**. Right now, you're not working for yourself more than a couple of hours a day while you're **awake**.

NARROWING YOUR SEARCH

As in all internet searches, the key is to narrow your search from the millions of job possibilities to the handful that will actually suit your needs and talents.

For example, some online sites or search engines will have you enter **keywords** to find your job. Be as honest and specific as you can. The best keywords provide information both about you and the kind of employment you're seeking.

KEYWORD

"**job**"

is too broad. But add:

"job and **high salary**"

and you've immediately eliminated literally millions of jobs that you don't want. Now further refine your search by adding:

"job and high salary and **upper management**"

You still may get thousands of responses, so you need to continue narrowing your search:

"job and high salary and upper management
and **benefits** and **three day work week**"

Now we're beginning to zero in on the most promising possibilities. Let's keep going:

"job and high salary and upper management and
benefits and three day work week and **beach**
and **sexy** and **rock 'n roll**"

If you're still receiving too many offers, you should add a few keywords about yourself:

"job and high salary and upper management and
benefits and three day work week and beach
and sexy and rock 'n roll and **college
graduate, lazy, unilingual**"

Now you have a specific, **targeted** job profile, broad enough to attract multiple job offers, but narrow enough to filter out the ones you wouldn't be interested in. Hit the "submit" icon and wait for the exciting results.

This may take a few minutes, so while you're waiting, why don't you move on to the next chapter?

CHAPTER 49:

Careers in Research: Body Parts You Can Live Without

Kidneys—You only really need one

Fingers—It's the opposable thumb that distinguishes us (and the apes) from other animals, like donkeys, so you'll definitely want to keep both of your thumbs. But what about your "ring finger?" Not really doing all that much, huh?

Toes—Expendable, but not much demand for them

Ears—One is all you need for most hearing situations

Eyes— Really good market for eyes, but helps to have two

Liver—Probably a keeper

Heart—A definite keeper

Lungs—Best keep these also, although you *do* have two

Spleen—Don't need it, but might not be able to sell it

Appendix—Ditto

172 THE DOG ATE MY RESUME

Sex Organs—Often more trouble than they're worth, but you'll miss them when they're gone

Of course the above is just a rough guideline. You probably have your own, personal favorite organs, and others you couldn't care less about. Feel free to adjust to your own, idiosyncratic taste.

SUMMARY FOR STUDENTS

While a career in research as suggested above can be interesting and lucrative, after you've sold your least favorite organs, the possibility for extending your career begins to diminish, so you'll want to have a backup career option as well.

SUMMARY FOR PARENTS

After paying for college, you may want to check out this exciting field as a supplement to your current work.

SECTION FIVE

COMMUNITY SERVICE: IF ALL ELSE FAILS, HELP THE NEEDY

CHAPTER 50:

THE PEACE CORPS: 10 DISEASES YOU'VE NEVER EVEN HEARD OF

The day-to-day, hands-in-the-dirt tasks you perform while overseas will be reward in and of themselves, but what is truly lasting are the things you take with you from this magical experience. These things include, but are not limited to:

1. Toxoplasmosis
2. Dengue
3. Leishmaniasis
4. Onchocerciasis
5. Trypanosomiasis
6. Schistosomiasis
7. Leptospirosis
8. Endophthalmitis
9. Coccidioidomycosis
10. Filariasis

SUMMARY FOR STUDENTS

What, you wanted more?

SUMMARY FOR PARENTS

Relax. Most of these diseases are preventable and/or treatable. Remember, you can't make an omelet without picking up the occasional intestinal parasite.

CHAPTER 51:

AMERICORPS: 10 LETHAL WEAPONS YOU'VE NEVER HEARD OF

We interrupt this chapter title to bring you this late-breaking update:

This chapter has been **canceled** due to lack of funding.

However, if you're interested in community service, see chapter on Careers in the **Military**, which recently received a lot of **additional funding**.

CHAPTER 52:

MAKING THE WORLD A BETTER PLACE, OR AT LEAST CLEANING YOUR APARTMENT

Making the world a better place is a pretty intimidating challenge, but one which you, today's graduate, will no doubt be hearing quite a lot about from speakers at your graduation. Most of these speakers will be members of your parents' generation. And guess what? They heard exactly the same thing from *their* commencement speakers. So let's check up and see how your parents' generation handled this challenge.

Positive Contributions of Your Parents' Generation	Negative Contributions
Won Cold War, defeated Evil Empire	Started our own Evil Empire
Began Era of Peace and Love	Ended Era of Peace and Love
Women's Liberation	*Charlie's Angels*
Drugs, Sex, Rock 'n' Roll	War on Drugs, Sex, Rock 'n' Roll
Put man on the moon	Put mochachino frappe in coffee
The Beatles	*The Brady Bunch*
"We Shall Overcome"	"Groovy"
Eradicated Polio	Created Bill O'Reilly

So you can see this record of world betterment is not going to be too hard to meet, and even exceed. This will give you the confidence you need to go out there and really make the world a better place, which you will need to do because:

Whether you have had all the strings pulled for you or have worked your ass off to get here, you now have a degree that fingers you as one of the top 1% of the world in power, education and the ability to effect change. Thus, changing the world is not your challenge in life but your **obligation** and **duty**. Think of all those people who have worked on your behalf all those years: teachers, parents, leaders. They will not only be pleased if you make the world a better place, they will be devastated if you don't. Their life's work was riding on the hope that you could take up where they left off.

If you fail, you bring down not only yourself and your family, but also every trash man, lunch lady, bus boy, janitor, teacher, and campus security guard who has not had the opportunities you have had, but nonetheless worked day and night to provide you with the things you have needed along your path to this point. Now you have the power to correct the injustices these people have long struggled against, but been unable to rectify. But if you fail, their entire existence becomes meaningless. In short, any of your successes are really *their* successes, while your failures are yours alone, yet will have catastrophic consequences rippling through history, dismantling the delicate fabric which created you and destroying all **hope** for a better **future.**

Summary for Students

You could at least vote.

Summary for Parents

Let's be honest: you didn't actually leave the world a better place. Adding the positives and subtracting the negatives, it's at best a wash. But you can still insist that your children's generation make the world better. Somebody should do it. To instill in them the motivation to change the world, you can use the very same tools you have used so effectively in raising them to this point of achievement in their lives, that is: guilt, shame, a sense of obligation, and a fear of failure. They certainly can't screw it up any worse than you did.

FiNAL EXAM

1. Why is Journalism not covered in this book?

A) Anonymous, high-ranking sources say authors couldn't think of anything funny to say about journalism.

B) Other, higher-ranking sources, speaking off the record, dismissed these allegations as unsubstantiated rumors and speculation.

C) Actually, Fox News was mentioned three times. Are you saying that Fox News isn't journalism at its finest? Are you some kind of terrorist?

2. After reading the entire book, or skipping to the Final Exam, what is most disappointing about the book *now*?

A) The useful advice promised in the mid term exam never showed up.

B) I still don't have a decent job.

C) I still don't have a job.

3. Sociology is:

A) Psychology's evil twin.

B) Excellent preparation for graduate school in any other field.

C) The Bermuda Triangle of unemployment.

4. The most important method for getting that first big job is:

A) Maintaining a positive attitude.

B) Persevering in the face of inevitable setbacks.

C) Developing a network of friends and classmates.

D) Nepotism.

5. How come none of the questions on these tests are actually covered in the book?

A) This book is forward-looking, not backward-looking.

B) Real education is not measured by how many facts you can cram into your brain by popping No-Doz and staying up all night before the exam, but rather by the analytical skills you have learned by popping No-Doz and staying up all night before the exam.

C) It levels the playing field for those of you who didn't do the reading.

6. Due to grade inflation, the percentage of Harvard graduates in the top 1% of their graduating class this year is:

A) 6%

B) 28.5%

C) 100%

PART II: ESSAY QUESTION

A college education is the most important stepping-stone to the future. Citing specific examples from your personal experience, compare and contrast the skills and knowledge you've acquired reading, writing and researching, with the brain damage you've sustained drinking.

If you feel you've answered any of the above questions correctly, you get an A! (Harvard isn't the only place where there's been a little grade inflation.)

APPENDIX

FULL LIFE EXPERIENCE CHECK LIST

If you actually manage to find a career right after college, you may wonder what else is out there that you might be **missing**. If you're worried that your life has become too stable/predictable too early, fear not: it's never too late to do all the major, exciting life activities other people do or have done. Here is an exhaustive To Do List, which will ensure that you have done all the major things that humans are supposed to do to lead a full life.

—Sky dive (bungee jump, cliff dive)

—Jump into a pile of leaves

—Scuba dive off the Barrier Reef

—Drop in on a half pipe

—Knock over a house of cards

—Drive the wrong direction over those spikes that are supposed to cause "severe tire damage" to see if it really happens

—Visit Paris

—Build a snowman

—Read a book from cover to cover

—Outrun lava from a volcanic eruption

—Seek enlightenment in a Tibetan monastery

—Get bellybutton pierced

—Take some kids to a baseball game

—Streak a baseball game

—Streak a church

—Own a pony

—Ride on the back of a Giant Galapagos Turtle

—Get a hot-pink mohawk

—Learn to play the piccolo

—Join a religious cult

—Fight a tiger

—Ride a trapeze

—Get a job

—Start a forest fire

—Heckle musicians at a symphony orchestra

—Watch sunrise from the top of K-2

—Smash a large piece of machinery

—Slide down a fire pole

—Hunt your own dinner

Of course you don't have to do all 29 of the things on the Check List!

But if you don't do at least 28 of them, we can't be responsible for that crushing feeling of loss, squandered opportunity and suicidal despair which will overwhelm you when you look back with regret on your misspent life.

How to Succeed in Life: Writing Impressive Class Notes for the Alumni Magazine

In life, as in college, your success and satisfaction is measured not by what you actually manage to achieve, but by the **spin** you are able to put on it. In other words, what you write in the "Class Notes" section of your Alumni Magazine.

Since you have only just graduated, your first entries won't have to be terribly impressive, but it's never too soon to begin to embellish whatever it is you're doing so that you'll seem to be successful, and more importantly, your friends and classmates, by comparison, will seem to be **failures**.

Let us imagine that instead of moving swiftly into that first great job and career triumph, you've spent the better part of year one, post grad, **sponging** off your family and various friends, and possibly friends of friends. This is no reason not to submit a note to your class secretary for publication in the Alumni Bulletin. It might read:

> *YOUR NAME HERE is immersed in a comparative cultural anthropology field work study, comparing belief systems and social interactions of various ethnic groups and sub groups in contemporary YOUR GEOGRAPHICAL AREA HERE.*

While your classmates don't really need (or want) to hear about your progress every year, it's a good idea to keep them posted every five, or, at the most, ten years, lest they forget how **successful** you are, and by comparison, what **inferior** lives they are leading. After a suitable interval, you might check in with:

YOUR NAME HERE was married last spring to MADE UP NAME HERE, two weeks after she represented Brazil in the Miss South America Contest, which she won. She will have to postpone work on her Ph.D. thesis in biochemistry at the University of Sao Paulo in order to fulfill her obligation as a goodwill ambassador for the United Nations. YOUR NAME HERE will also be putting his career as a professional soccer player and psychotherapist on hold in order to support his new bride during her ambassadorial travels and erotic dance performances.

You can let that sink in for quite a few years, but sooner or later it will be time for another installment:

YOUR NAME HERE designed and built his own cliffside home in the Amazon rain forest, which was featured simultaneously in Beautiful Homes Magazine *and* Architectural Digest. *As soon as it was finished, he and his wife (the former Miss Brazil) moved in and wrote a memoir of their travels together as Goodwill Ambassadors for the United Nations and erotic dancers, which won the prestigious Christopher Columbus Award for Literature in Portuguese (over the strenuous objections of the Catholic Church). He hopes any classmates who happen to be traveling in the Amazon rain forest will drop by.*[27]

A good thing to keep in mind is that in writing these notes, less is more. Let your classmates begin to wonder what happened to you before checking in with:

---

[27]Don't worry, nobody will take you up on this offer.

After a bidding war broke out among the larger publishing houses for Adventures in the Amazon Rain Forest, *the sequel to their first book, YOUR NAME HERE and his wife, the former Miss Brazil,[28] were able to retire, giving the bulk of their advance to the indigenous peoples of the rain forest. He was then invited to an unnamed South Pacific island to start their space program, rekindling a childhood interest in rocketry. The launch of their first communications satellite was successful, rescuing the island from the threat of poverty, for which he was made the first honorary member of the Royal Family.*

That should keep them in the proper state of envy, until it's time for:

YOUR NAME HERE writes that his son, YOUR NAME HERE, JR., has just graduated magna cum laude *from Harvard, and is choosing between a Rhodes and a Fulbright Scholarship. His daughter, MADE UP NAME HERE, was elected Governor of Jalisco, Mexico, the youngest governor of Jalisco on record, and the first woman governor.*

The main thing is to keep your achievements sufficiently far removed from places your classmates are likely to live in or know about so that they (your achievements) remain credible.

SUMMARY FOR STUDENTS

The whole point of the "Class Notes" section in your Alumni Magazine is to engender an intense sense of **envy** in your classmates, and, if at all possible, an even more intense sense of **self-loathing** as well.

SUMMARY FOR PARENTS

It's **never too late** to make your classmates hate themselves as they contemplate your superior life. If you haven't managed to do this with your own or your children's lives, you still have your grandchildren's lives.

---

[28]In case they've forgotten.

THE INDIVIDUALLY CUSTOMIZED, NONDENOMINATIONALLY SPECIFIC HOLIDAY NETWORKING CARD TEMPLATE

Peace
Paix
Frieden
Irini
Shalom
Pace
Heiwa
Shanti
Sula
Pokoj
Paz
Runyaro
Mire
Fred
Sag
Khotso
Sidi

Dear _____,
*   While adding festive holiday decorations to my home, I thought of you. I was recalling with fondness the time we spent together _____ing at _____, way back in _____. Can you get me a job?*
*   All my best wishes,*

*   _____*

INDEX

B
Bank account, Russian mafia now has access to your 98
Boss, desire to kill your last 22
Borneo, orangutans in 51
Box, Jack in the 17
Bunny, Bugs 104
Busy, all of our technical support operators are 97

C
Contraire, au 92

D
Days, Good Old 93, 99, 101
Drugs, massive quantities of 26

E
Electrical socket, sticking your finger in an 84
Employed, why aren't you 53
Extradition treaties, countries with no 72

G
Guns, Operation Shooting People with 90
Guns, please do not come to our house with 117

H
Hit, price of 126
Humanity, oppressing and enslaving vast majority of 82

I
Inspirational Quotes, better, deeper, more advanced 44
Inspirational Quotes, regular 44

J
Job, shouldn't you already have a 13

L
Last guy, better than the 141
Last guy, what happened to the 167
Life, meaning of 47
Lottery, winning the 158–160

N
Nonprofit, working for a (see "Begging") 162–163
Nothing, doing 147–150

O
Overwork, early death due to 93

R
Repetition, technique of repeated 159–160
Representation, hegemonizing identity while reconstructing 136
Robbery, armed (see: Back Cover—author biographies)

S
Satan, capitulation to 55

T
Tables, waiting 12, 151–153
Things, undoing, that other people who do things have done 147
Tranquilizers, horse 107
Traveling (see "Doing Nothing") 148
Twinkies, fried 83

U
Unemployment, Bermuda Triangle of 178
Urges, homicidal 156

V
Voice, loud screaming 122

W
World, the real 15
World, The Real (TV show) 15

BOOKS AVAILABLE FROM SANTA MONICA PRESS

Blues for Bird
by Martin Gray
288 pages $16.95

The Book of Good Habits
Simple and Creative Ways to Enrich Your Life
by Dirk Mathison
224 pages $9.95

The Butt Hello
and other ways my cats drive me crazy
by Ted Meyer
96 pages $9.95

Café Nation
Coffee Folklore, Magick, and Divination
by Sandra Mizumoto Posey
224 pages $9.95

Cats Around the World
by Ted Meyer
96 pages $9.95

Childish Things
by Davis & Davis
96 pages $19.95

Discovering the History of Your House
and Your Neighborhood
by Betsy J. Green
288 pages $14.95

The Dog Ate My Resumé
by Zack Arnstein and Larry Arnstein
192 pages $11.95

Dogme Uncut
Lars von Trier, Thomas Vinterberg and the Gang That Took on Hollywood
by Jack Stevenson
312 pages $16.95

Exotic Travel Destinations for Families
by Jennifer M. Nichols and Bill Nichols
360 pages $16.95

Footsteps in the Fog
Alfred Hitchcock's San Francisco
by Jeff Kraft and Aaron Leventhal
240 pages $24.95

Free Stuff & Good Deals for Folks over 50, 2nd Ed.
by Linda Bowman
240 pages $12.95

How to Find Your Family Roots and Write Your Family History
by William Latham and Cindy Higgins
288 pages $14.95

How to Speak Shakespeare
by Cal Pritner and Louis Colaianni
144 pages $16.95

How to Win Lotteries, Sweepstakes, and Contests in the 21st Century
by Steve "America's Sweepstakes King" Ledoux
224 pages $14.95

Jackson Pollock: Memories Arrested in Space
by Martin Gray
216 pages $14.95

James Dean Died Here
The Locations of America's Pop Culture Landmarks
by Chris Epting
312 pages $16.95

The Keystone Kid
Tales of Early Hollywood
by Coy Watson, Jr.
312 pages $24.95

Letter Writing Made Easy!
Featuring Sample Letters for Hundreds of Common Occasions
by Margaret McCarthy
224 pages $12.95

Letter Writing Made Easy! Volume 2
Featuring More Sample Letters for Hundreds of Common Occasions
by Margaret McCarthy
224 pages $12.95

Life is Short. Eat Biscuits!
by Amy Jordan Smith
96 pages $9.95

Marilyn Monroe Dyed Here
More Locations of America's Pop Culture Landmarks
by Chris Epting
312 pages $16.95

Movie Star Homes
by Judy Artunian and Mike Oldham
312 pages $16.95

Offbeat Food
Adventures in an Omnivorous World
by Alan Ridenour
240 pages $19.95

Offbeat Marijuana
The Life and Times of the World's Grooviest Plant
by Saul Rubin
240 pages $19.95

Offbeat Museums
The Collections and Curators of America's Most Unusual Museums
by Saul Rubin
240 pages $19.95

A Prayer for Burma
by Kenneth Wong
216 pages $14.95

Quack!
Tales of Medical Fraud from the Museum of Questionable Medical Devices
by Bob McCoy
240 pages $19.95

Redneck Haiku
by Mary K. Witte
112 pages $9.95

School Sense: How to Help Your Child Succeed in Elementary School
by Tiffani Chin, Ph.D.
408 pages $16.95

Silent Echoes
Discovering Early Hollywood Through the Films of Buster Keaton
by John Bengtson
240 pages $24.95

Tiki Road Trip
A Guide to Tiki Culture in North America
by James Teitelbaum
288 pages $16.95

SANTA
MONICA
PRESS

ORDER FORM 1-800-784-9553

	Quantity	Amount
Blues for Bird (epic poem about Charlie Parker) ($16.95)	————	————
The Book of Good Habits ($9.95)	————	————
The Butt Hello . . . and Other Ways My Cats Drive Me Crazy ($9.95)	————	————
Café Nation: Coffee Folklore, Magick and Divination ($9.95)	————	————
Cats Around the World ($9.95)	————	————
Childish Things ($19.95)	————	————
Discovering the History of Your House. . . ($14.95)	————	————
The Dog Ate My Resumé ($11.95)	————	————
Dogme Uncut ($16.95)	————	————
Exotic Travel Destinations for Families ($16.95)	————	————
Footsteps in the Fog: Alfred Hitchcock's San Francisco ($24.95)	————	————
Free Stuff & Good Deals for Folks over 50, 2nd Ed. ($12.95)	————	————
How to Find Your Family Roots . . . ($14.95)	————	————
How to Speak Shakespeare ($16.95)	————	————
How to Win Lotteries, Sweepstakes, and Contests . . . ($14.95)	————	————
Jackson Pollock: Memories Arrested in Space ($14.95)	————	————
James Dean Died Here: America's Pop Culture Landmarks ($16.95)	————	————
The Keystone Kid: Tales of Early Hollywood ($24.95)	————	————
Letter Writing Made Easy! ($12.95)	————	————
Letter Writing Made Easy! Volume 2 ($12.95)	————	————
Life is Short. Eat Biscuits! ($9.95)	————	————
Marilyn Monroe Dyed Here ($16.95)	————	————
Movie Star Homes ($16.95)	————	————
Offbeat Food ($19.95)	————	————
Offbeat Marijuana ($19.95)	————	————
Offbeat Museums ($19.95)	————	————
A Prayer for Burma ($14.95)	————	————
Quack! Tales of Medical Fraud ($19.95)	————	————
Redneck Haiku ($9.95)	————	————
School Sense ($16.95)	————	————
Silent Echoes: Early Hollywood Through Buster Keaton ($24.95)	————	————
Tiki Road Trip ($16.95)	————	————

		Subtotal	————
Shipping & Handling:		CA residents add 8.25% sales tax	————
1 book $3.00		Shipping and Handling (see left)	————
Each additional book is $ .50		**TOTAL**	————

Name ————————————————————————————————

Address ——————————————————————————————

City ———————————————— State ———————— Zip ——————————

❑ Visa ❑ MasterCard   Card No.: —————————————————————

Exp. Date ———————————— Signature ——————————————————

❑ Enclosed is my check or money order payable to:

Santa Monica Press LLC
P.O. Box 1076
Santa Monica, CA 90406
www.santamonicapress.com 1-800-784-9553